Whodunit Puzzles

*Brainteasers
from Riddle
Middle
School*

Robert Mandelberg

Sterling Publishing Co., Inc.
New York

To Eliana and Nika: My beautiful baby and her beautiful mommy.

A special thanks to Jeff Horak, Marty Horak, Julius Rosenthal, Karen Cook, and Rodman P. Neumann.

Other Books by Robert Mandelberg
Easy Mind-Reading Tricks
The Case of the Curious Campaign: A Whodunit of Many Mini-Mysteries
Mystifying Mind Reading Tricks
Mind-Reading Card Tricks

Book Design: Rae Grant

Library of Congress Cataloging-in-Publication Data
         Mandelberg, Robert.
Whodunit puzzles : brainteasers from Riddle Middle School / Robert Mandelberg.
     p. cm.
Includes index.
ISBN-13: 978-1-4027-2453-4
ISBN-10: 1-4027-2453-5
1. Puzzles. 2. Detective and mystery stories. I. Title.

GV1507.D4M36 2006
793.73--dc22

          2006002557

10 9 8 7 6 5 4 3 2 1

Published by Sterling Publishing Co., Inc.
387 Park Avenue South, New York, NY 10016
© 2006 by Robert Mandelberg
Distributed in Canada by Sterling Publishing
c/o Canadian Manda Group, One Atlantic Avenue, Suite 105
Toronto, Ontario, Canada M6K 3E7
Distributed in the United Kingdom by GMC Distribution Services,
Castle Place, 166 High Street, Lewes, East Sussex, England BN7 1XU
Distributed in Australia by Capricorn Link (Australia) Pty. Ltd.
P.O. Box 704, Windsor, NSW 2756 Australia

Manufactured in the United States of America

Sterling ISBN-13: 978-1-4027-2453-4
      ISBN-10: 1-4027-2453-5

For information about custom editions, special sales, premium and corporate purchases, please contact Sterling Special Sales Department at 800-805-5489 or specialsales@sterlingpub.com.

Contents

Whodunit Puzzles

Brainteasers from Riddle Middle School

The tension was thick in the faculty conference room that Tuesday morning at Riddle Middle School. The principal, Graham Marshall, had called an emergency meeting with all of his head teachers. The last time such a meeting took place was eight years earlier, when there was a school scandal and half the teachers were fired. Recalling that fateful day, the head teachers sat nervously around the conference table awaiting the arrival of Principal Marshall.

It was 6:30 A.M. and all present were confused and groggy, still trying to shake the morning sleep out of their heads. Carrie Cook, the head of the math department, sipped her French vanilla coffee. With each sip, she lifted the cup carefully to her lips, blew on the hot liquid, and drew in the steam, until the coffee slurped into her mouth; then she gulped loudly and slowly exhaled. *Lift, blow, slurp, gulp, exhale.* Over and over. Each new round of sipping grated on the nerves of everyone at the table.

To Mrs. Cook's left sat Bob Raccoon, the head of the science department. A quiet loner with poor eyesight, Mr. Raccoon heartily munched on a chocolate éclair, carelessly smearing streaks of icing on his chin, giving himself a chocolate beard. He closely guarded two other éclairs that were sitting on a small napkin in front of him. Normally, Mr. Raccoon preferred eating candy bars for breakfast. And he liked his chocolate messy—the gooier the better. But due to a recent break-in, the vending machines were completely empty. Someone had apparently snuck into the faculty dining room and stolen all the candy, forcing Mr. Raccoon to switch to pastries from the local donut shop.

To the left of Mr. Raccoon was Mike Magnesium, the five-foot-one-inch vice principal who had been with the school for 17 years. A notoriously bad dresser, Vice Principal Magnesium wore a pair of dark green slacks that were so short, it seemed as if he were expecting the bathroom pipes to burst and flood the hallways.

Vice Principal Magnesium was feeling out of sorts this morning because he hadn't had time to eat breakfast. He swirled his thumbs in rapid circles and jealously eyed Mr. Raccoon's spare pastries. From his belly came a low growl. Hearing this, Mr. Raccoon inched his spare chocolate éclairs closer to his body for protection.

Across the table sat Nicole Stewart, who was in charge of the social studies department. With no teaching experience and a complete lack of understanding of history, geography, current events, or any other social study, Miss Stewart caused the other teachers to wonder who in her family sat on the Board of Education to get her a job as a social studies teacher. Miss Stewart stared at herself in a small hand mirror, as she thought about whether or not to have her hair highlighted. After much consideration, she decided against it.

To Miss Stewart's left sat Morey Holland, the head of the theater department. All of the students and most of the teachers were too young to remember that Morey Holland once starred in the *Watch My Garden Grow* TV show in the 1960s. Unable to find work as a comedian, Mr. Holland used his semi-celebrity status to bully the superintendent into giving him a teaching position. But Morey's constant jokes and cries of "I used to be big" caused Principal Marshall to regret the day he agreed to allow him into the school.

Finally, to Mr. Holland's left, sat Sophie Turkus, head of the English department. With a master's degree from Harvard, a Ph.D. from Yale, and a certificate of completion from the Valvo School of Refrigerator Repair, Mrs. Turkus was by far the most brilliant member of the staff. She was the one person who could be relied upon to solve the school's hardest problems and keep the mini-fridge in the faculty dining room up and running.

The head teachers sat in complete silence, except for the occasional slurps of Mrs. Cook's coffee and a soft humming coming from Mr. Raccoon as he enjoyed his pastries. Then, without warning, the door to the conference room burst open. All heads turned to see Principal Marshall enter. Principal Graham Marshall was an imposing figure, standing six-feet-four-inches tall, with a thick, black moustache and a muscular build. He looked angry as he strode to the front of the conference table. Principal Marshall surveyed the room, scanning the faces of his trembling department heads.

Although one would expect a booming, commanding voice to come from someone so big and strong, Principal Marshall spoke in a high-pitched tone, rumored to be due to a birth defect. "Heads are going to roll," he cried out, the tone eerily unbefitting the powerful 51-year-old school principal.

This was exactly how it had started eight years ago, right before all the firings took place. Morey Holland tried to keep cool, but couldn't stop a tear from streaking down his left cheek. The former television star needed this job more than the others did. If he got fired, he would have to go back to signing autographs at Taco Bell openings amid a sea of voices pondering, "Morey who?" The other department heads looked away, also scared that they were about to lose their jobs.

"We're on the brink of disaster!" screeched the principal. "As all of you know, a lot of eighth-graders have been skipping school lately. To show that this will not be tolerated, I have issued suspensions to more than 150 students. But it seems that some of these students refuse to take their suspensions without a fight. When I got to my office this morning, I found a handwritten note on my desk."

The principal pulled a piece of paper from his pocket, put on his glasses, and read the contents to his staff:

Dear Principal Marshall:

Guess what? Me and my friend have stolen all of the midterm exams! It was so much fun watching my friend hacking into the computer and printing the exams—hehehe. At first, one of us hid the exams in the boys' locker room while changing for gym, but they're in a much safer place now. You'll never find them! Maybe this will make you think twice before you suspend all of us and get us in trouble with our parents. Unless you IMMEDIATELY drop the suspensions, we will give out the tests to all the students. Did you think we wouldn't do anything about it? We're smart eighth graders! What did you take us for? A bunch of seventh graders?

Principal Marshall slammed the note down on the table and surveyed his staff. "So, it looks like there were two students who stole the tests. Any thoughts on who they could be?"

The department heads looked at each other perplexed. Finally, Sophie Turkus, head of the English department, spoke up. "It couldn't have been any of my students."

"And why not?" asked the principal.

"Because the note said, 'Me and my friend...' My students would have known to write, 'My friend and I,'" replied Mrs. Turkus smugly.

Principal Marshall dismissed the comment and continued to address his staff: "I do not know who stole the exams, but I can tell you this: First, I am not reversing any suspensions. And second, I will not allow these tests to be distributed to the students."

Vice Principal Magnesium stood and said, "But if you won't give in to their demands, how will you stop them from distributing the tests?"

Principal Marshall mimicked Mr. Magnesium with savage sarcasm, "But if you won't give in to their demands..." He shot an angry look at Vice Principal Magnesium and then continued:

"That is precisely why I gathered you here today. All of you have enjoyed special privileges as senior staff members. And for what? You're nothing but a bunch of mealymouthed, has-been know-it-alls. If the six of you want to continue as department heads, you will find the culprits who stole the exams by tomorrow! Do I make myself clear?"

He paused to scrutinize his staff's reactions. It was nearly impossible for the quivering teachers to keep eye contact with Principal Marshall as he stood at the front of the table, glowering at them one by one.

The department heads all signaled their understanding, except for Mr. Raccoon, who continued to chomp merrily on his pastry, completely unaware of the seriousness of the matter.

Principal Marshall reached over the table, grabbed Mr. Raccoon's last éclair, and squeezed it in his massive hand. The school principal gritted his teeth, as the gooey contents oozed through his fingers. He then wiped his hand on Mr. Raccoon's tie, while fixing his gaze on him. "Am I making myself clear, Mr. Raccoon?" he asked sternly. Mr. Raccoon looked terrified as he nodded in agreement.

"Good! Just as I wasn't afraid to suspend 150 eighth-graders, I will not be afraid to demote every last one of you," he said, now looking around the table. "We've got to crack this case by tomorrow. Don't let me down." Then the principal was gone, slamming the door behind him.

The department heads looked at one another and then spent the next few minutes trying to come up with a plan to find out who stole the exams. For the time being, they decided to work separately to see what they could discover.

✳✳✳

The story continues with 19 Whodunit Puzzles, as Vice Principal Magnesium begins his investigation in the computer lab—see Challenge 1—The Racquet Brothers.

1. The Racquet Brothers

Vice Principal Magnesium decided to start his inquiry in the computer lab, since all of the midterm exams were stored on the school's network. He wanted to see if any of the students had been tampering with the system. On his way to the lab, he shuddered because he knew that he would soon encounter Bill and Nick Racquet, Riddle Middle School's computer teachers.

Vice Principal Magnesium had been curious about Bill and Nick Racquet ever since they started teaching at Riddle Middle School five years ago. The two men were brothers and looked 100 percent alike. It was impossible to tell them apart physically. Not only were they an exact mirror image of each other, but they also shared the same mannerisms. With a liking for striped suits and flowery ties, the Racquet brothers even dressed alike. But here is why Vice Principal Magnesium was so curious: Although they were identical in appearance, Bill and Nick Racquet were *not* twins.

The vice principal had decided that the Racquet brothers' uncanny resemblance to each other was simply a freak coincidence and that the two brothers must have been born less than a year apart. He had thought that right up until the time he happened to be reviewing their personnel records. As vice principal, Mr. Magnesium was able to see all of the teachers' confidential files. He had been startled to learn that Bill and Nick were not born a year apart, as he had thought initially, but were, in fact, both born on February 12th of the *exact same year*.

He had wondered if they, perchance, shared the same father but had different mothers. After checking around, this theory was struck down when he learned that Bill and Nick had the same birth parents.

This drove Vice Principal Magnesium mad. He wracked his brain to come up with a possible explanation, but he could not. So whenever he saw the Racquet brothers, he asked himself the same question:

If the two men were born on the exact same day of the exact same year and had the exact same parents, how is it possible that they were not twins? (*Solution on page 80.*)

2. True or False

Yes, physically, Bill and Nick Racquet were identical. However, there was one trait that set the two brothers apart: While Bill Racquet was always honest, his brother was the complete opposite. Nick Racquet was a compulsive liar, incapable of saying anything truthful.

For those who understood Nick, it was often amusing to speak with him. He would try his best to answer questions with the exact opposite of the truth. And sometimes that was difficult. For example, if it was Monday and someone asked Nick what day it was, he had to struggle to find the answer that was furthest away from the truth. And what's the opposite of Monday? Nick decided that it was Friday, since they are on opposite ends of the school week. Another example: Nick owns a German shepherd named Kippy. One time a student asked Nick if he had any pets. One might imagine that a liar would simply answer "No." But Nick was more complex than that. He said that he had a *cat* named Kippy. You see, in Nick's mind, cat was the opposite of dog.

With his pattern of blatantly lying at every opportunity, it was a wonder that Nick was still allowed to work at the school. The truth was that his coworkers found Nick to be fun and quirky, and they had grown accustomed to converting everything he said to the opposite. The only problem was distinguishing Bill and Nick from each other.

Vice Principal Magnesium arrived at the computer lab, and, as he had predicted, Bill and Nick Racquet were standing by the front door. "Good morning, Vice Principal Magnesium," the brothers said in unison.

"Good morning, Bill, Nick," replied the vice principal, not sure who was whom. From his pocket, VP Magnesium pulled out a key ring with two keys. He studied the keys for a moment and realized that he did not know which key opened the computer lab. It was important that the wrong key was not put into the lock, because this would set off the school alarm system and the police would be swarming all over the building within minutes. He could ask one of the brothers which key was correct, but what good was that if he couldn't tell which one was telling the truth?

Vice Principal Magnesium studied both men closely, trying to figure out which brother had "lying eyes." He wanted to discern which brother was Bill, since he would be sure that Bill would tell the truth. Vice Principal Magnesium also realized that it would be equally as helpful if he identified Nick, as he could then convert anything Nick said to the opposite. But which one was which? The vice principal decided to try a direct approach. He stepped back and said, "Which one of you is Bill?"

"I am," said Bill and Nick simultaneously.

"Hmm," uttered the vice principal. "That didn't work. Let me try again. Which one of you tells the truth?"

"I do," said the brothers, again in unison.

Vice Principal Magnesium was beginning to understand that this was going to be harder than he thought. "Which of these keys will open the computer lab?"

"This one," they answered, each pointing to different keys.

"No," he said in frustration. "I need to open the computer lab. This isn't a joke. Now, which key opens the room?"

Again the Racquet brothers pointed to different keys. Vice Principal Magnesium began to pace. He knew that the only way this would work is if he asked the men a question that would make them point to the same key. But what could it be? He pondered:

What <u>one</u> question could he ask either brother that would identify the proper key? (*Solution on page 80.*)

3. Rodman Pilgrim

Rodman Pilgrim chose an unfortunate day to begin his first day of school at Riddle Middle. Oh, how he despised being the "new kid" yet again! Over the past seven years, Rodman has had to be the new kid in five different schools. His father would get one job after another, which meant they always had to pack up and move.

Rodman knew the routine: He would sit by himself for the first few weeks before he had an opportunity to make friends. But as soon as he started to fit in, he would find out that his family had to move again. He had been through this many times. Nonetheless, the eighth-grader still wanted to make a good impression.

Rodman's mother dropped him off at the front of the school. By the time he checked in with the office and made his way to his classroom, it was already 20 minutes into second period. "Oh great," Rodman uttered to himself. "Now I can't just slip into class at the beginning—I have to walk in late and have everyone stare at me." Fortunately for Rodman, this was his Advanced Placement English class, which had only four other students.

When Rodman arrived at the class, he was surprised to find it empty. Everyone must be at an assembly or something, he thought. Although he wasn't expecting a large banner saying "Welcome Aboard Rodman," he had hoped that there would at least be a teacher there to greet him and show him where to sit. But there wasn't a trace of anyone in sight. He stood in the doorway looking at five empty desks. All he wanted to do was to put down his books and get settled, but he didn't know which desk was his. The last thing that Rodman needed was to get himself in hot water on the first day of his new school by taking someone else's seat. He sighed heavily.

After a few moments, Rodman heard someone whistling a happy but off-key tune from down the hallway. Stepping into the corridor, he saw a stocky, gray-haired gentleman carrying a large mop and roaming the hall. It was the school custodian, Mr. Pock. Rodman approached him timidly.

"Excuse me, sir. I am new here. My name is Rodman Pilgrim."

"Pilgrim?" queried the old man. "Stan and Marlene's son?"

"No," said Rodman apologetically. "Today is my first day, and I am having trouble locating my desk. I was wondering if you could assist me."

"Well, I don't know anything about desks. I'm the janitor. Have been for the past 40 years. But for Stan and Marlene's kid, I'll try my best."

"My parents are Keith and Roberta," insisted Rodman. "But I would really appreciate any help you could give me."

The aged janitor and earnest eighth-grader walked to the empty classroom. The old man looked around at the five chairs and stroked his chin. He said, "Well, let's see. Some things I know and some things I don't know. I can only tell you the things I know. But maybe from the things I know, the things I don't know can be known. Ya know?"

Rodman's head started to spin, and a spot of drool appeared in the corner of his mouth, but he was fairly confident that he understood. "I think so," ventured Rodman.

The custodian said, "Fine. Let's see. There are four students in this class: Fran Doyle, Gilbert Dwyer, Peter Nickels, and Gordon Reed. And there are five desks, so the empty one must be yours. Okay, here's what I can remember:

1. Fran is not at desk number 1.
2. Gilbert sits next to the empty desk.
3. Fran is two desks away from Peter.
4. Fran sits next to the empty desk.
5. Peter sits at desk number 4.

"Did that help?" asked the old man.

Rodman looked cross-eyed, as he tried to work out the seating arrangements in his head. After a moment, he felt something spark in his brain. Raising his finger, he said, "*Yes!* That was an enormous help. Thank you very much." Rodman then walked over to his desk and sat down.

Which desk was Rodman's? Where do the others sit? (*Solution on page 81.*)

4. A Safe Solution

Rodman Pilgrim took his class schedule out of the envelope and saw that his next class was math with Mrs. Cook in room C-19. He put the schedule back in the envelope and sighed. Unfortunately for Rodman, most of the classrooms were not numbered and none of them seemed to start with a letter. The bell had already rung a few minutes before, and Rodman became anxious at the thought of arriving at his class so late. After walking aimlessly down the hall searching for classroom C-19, Rodman was still clueless.

Just as he was about to give up, he saw a girl turn the corner and walk straight toward him. It was Ashleigh Ray, the school's head cheerleader. She was blonde, pretty, and destined to be a Homecoming Queen. Ashleigh was so popular that there was a waiting list a page long just to sit at her lunch table. Rodman could tell even from way down the hall that this girl was out of his league. He had always been far too shy to ever approach a girl—especially one like Ashleigh—but he needed to get to class and there was no one else to ask. *Oh, please don't let me say anything stupid,* thought Rodman over and over as she drew nearer.

When Ashleigh was within speaking distance, Rodman sucked in his gut, took a deep breath, and said . . . nothing. Not hello, I need to find C-19, nice day, not anything. He just stood there looking helpless. For some reason, Rodman held out his envelope, hoping Ashleigh would somehow know that this meant he was lost. Ashleigh stopped for a moment, looked at Rodman, and looked at the envelope. Then Ashleigh took the envelope from

Rodman's outstretched hand and continued on her way down the hall. When she was gone, Rodman exhaled and kicked himself for not being able to summon the courage to ask her where the classroom was.

Now Rodman was in even worse shape than before: He was completely lost and with no class schedule. His last remaining option was to walk into a classroom and ask a teacher for directions. To Rodman, the only thing more embarrassing than barging into his class late on his first day was barging into a class that wasn't his on his first day to ask for directions. Way to make a great first impression, he thought.

He nervously approached the next room down the hall, timidly opened the door, and stepped inside. It was Mr. Raccoon's science class. Upon entering, he immediately wished he had chosen a different room. He wanted to retreat, but it was too late.

At the front of the classroom, Mr. Raccoon was conversing with two students. They were in the middle of a very heated discussion. One student, named Alex Silvers, was tall and skinny with curly black hair. He was wearing a basketball shirt with the team's name on it: The Riddle Spiders. Alex was the star center on the school's basketball team.

The other student, named Rudy Wichter, was much shorter with spiked hair and two bushy eyebrows that joined in the middle. If that wasn't enough to make him stand out in a crowd, Rudy also had both hands in casts. And not the soft cloth casts either. Both hands and all his fingers were fully encased inside hard plastic. Unbeknownst to Rodman, Rudy was also on the school's basketball team and had sprained both hands two weeks earlier when he dove for a loose ball.

Definitely eighth-graders, Rodman thought. On the teacher's desk was a small, black safe. Beakers and Bunsen burners were on tables throughout the room. Must be in the science lab, Rodman surmised.

Seeing the teacher and the two students huddled together, Rodman suddenly thought of them as the "Three Amigos." They were speaking in half-whispers, indicating that they did not want anyone to hear what they were saying. Rodman felt like an unwanted intruder. He remained perfectly still, hoping that they wouldn't look up and see him standing there.

While he tried to figure a way out of the classroom, he heard the teacher say, "I'm going to keep the key. This way I can be sure that neither of you will empty out the safe when I'm not around."

Alex frowned. "I don't think that will work," he replied." How do we know *you* won't empty it out when *we're* not around? I think it's best that I hold onto the safe key for safekeeping."

The teacher and Rudy didn't like that suggestion. Soon, the three were arguing back and forth to see who would be the keeper of the key.

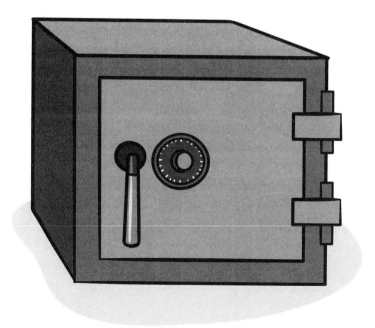

Finally, the teacher said, "Since we don't trust each other, we are going to have to find a solution where the only way the safe can be opened is if at least two of us are there at the same time. That way, none of us can sneak off and open the safe behind the others' backs."

"Yeah, but how can we make that happen?" asked Alex.

"I'm not sure exactly," replied the teacher, "but we will have to use more than one lock and one key."

Rudy asked, "Can we get as many keys and locks as we need?"

"Yes," replied the teacher. "But keys and locks are expensive, so we have to use the least number of keys and locks possible."

As the teacher and the two students were scratching their heads and rubbing their chins trying to come up with a solution, Rodman began slowly backing away toward the door. Because he wasn't looking where he was going, he accidentally knocked his leg into a table, which caused a beaker to teeter, spin, and fall to the floor, bursting into a million tiny chards in all directions.

It took less than a second for the three of them to turn their heads and catch Rodman trying to tiptoe out of the classroom. "*Hold it!*" barked the teacher. "Who are you? What are you doing here? Did Principal Marshall send you here to spy on us?"

"No, no, nothing like that!" Rodman replied. He quickly explained that he was lost and looking for Mrs. Cook's math class in room C-19.

The Three Amigos surrounded Rodman. There was no way he could escape now, he thought.

"How long were you standing there?" Alex asked, peering down at him.

"Did you hear us taking about the safe?" asked Rudy, inching closer.

"Because we have nothing of interest in the safe," added the teacher, looking worried.

"Yeah, nothing," said Alex. "Just some . . . just some . . . items, that's all."

"Yeah, items," echoed Rudy. "Nothing to go running to Principal Marshall about."

Rodman began sweating buckets and shaking. He said, "Yes, of course. Some items. I believe you." Rodman didn't believe them. They didn't believe Rodman. He was in a pickle. Thinking fast, Rodman said, "Well, um, I think I can help you with your science experiment."

"Experiment? What experiment is that?" asked the teacher.

"You know, the experiment with the locks and keys: to find the least number of locks and keys needed so that any two of you could open the safe together—but none of you could open it alone."

"Oh yes, of course, *that* experiment," remarked Rudy, now convinced that Rodman thought they were doing a class project. "Well? What's your solution?" asked the teacher.

What was Rodman's solution? (*Solution on page 85.*)

5. Thermos Be a Better Way

Meanwhile, clear across the school in the C-Wing, Mrs. Cook was enjoying her mid-mid-afternoon coffee. This was one of her favorite cups of the day, because it helped fill the long gap between her early-mid-afternoon cup and her late-mid-afternoon cup. She slowly brought the cup from the saucer to her mouth to begin her sipping ritual: *Lift, blow, slurp, gulp, exhale . . . Lift, blow, slurp, gulp, exhale.* Although her students were starting to file into the classroom, her eyes remained fixed on her cup of java.

"Good afternoon, class," began the math teacher, now looking up from her coffee. "Today's assignment will not only test your math skills, but it will also help me with a personal problem. As you may have noticed, on occasion I enjoy a nice hot cup of coffee. But what you may not know is that I drink my coffee 10 ounces at a time. Not 9.9 ounces, not 10.1 ounces, but exactly 10 ounces. If I drink even the slightest amount less than 10 ounces, I do not get my fill of coffee. And if I drink more than 10 ounces, I start to shake from the caffeine."

The class sat in silence wondering why Mrs. Cook was droning on about her coffee-drinking habits. She paused to savor the last gulp of her mid-mid-afternoon coffee. The last gulp was always a sad one for Mrs. Cook, because it meant that she had to wait a full 55 minutes before her next cup. *Lift, blow, slurp, gulp.* . . and this time, instead of exhale, it was more of a sighhhh.

"So here is my dilemma," she told her students. "Yesterday, I chipped my 10-ounce coffee Thermos. Although I hate to be apart from it, I had no choice but to bring it into the shop for repairs. Unfortunately, they did not have another 10-ounce

Thermos to give me as a loaner while mine was being serviced. Instead, they gave me three other Thermoses: 7 ounces, 9 ounces, and 11 ounces. The coffee machine in the back of the classroom can make unlimited amounts of coffee, but I need to find a way I can pour exactly 10 ounces."

Mrs. Cook continued: "Right now I'm drinking out of the 11-ounce thermos, and quite frankly I believe I poured a little too much and I'll be shaking like a lunatic in a few minutes. This is why it's important that someone figure out a way to fill exactly 10 ounces. Whoever devises the best solution will be given extra credit. Does everyone understand the assignment?"

Mrs. Cook looked around the class and saw her students nodding in agreement. "Well, sharpen your pencils and get to work. Let me know when you have something."

As soon as her students opened their notebooks, Mrs. Cook peered longingly into her empty Thermos, mentally calculating the amount of time left before her next cup of sweet heaven. Before she could sink too deeply into her coffee reverie, she noticed a slight commotion in the front row.

Looking up, she found Lori-Beth Sugarman, the know-it-all teacher's pet, straining her arm as high as she could. As her hand moved frantically, a grunting sound escaped her lips. Lori-Beth was a girl who got straight A's in every class, but had no social skills whatsoever. She did not have a single friend in the entire school. Lori-Beth continued to wave her hand until Mrs. Cook called on her. "Yes, Lori-Beth?" said the teacher.

"I have the answer, Mrs. Cook," said Lori-Beth with a look of superiority on her face. The other students shrugged and slapped their pencils down on their desks in disappointment. Her smug attitude was one of the primary reasons that Lori-Beth was unable to make friends.

"That was fast, Lori-Beth. Show me."

Lori-Beth stood up and walked haughtily to Mrs. Cook's desk.

She picked up the 11-ounce Thermos, carried it to the back of the room, and set it down next to the two other Thermoses. "It's so simple. Watch."

With a wide, toothy grin, Lori-Beth placed the 11-ounce Thermos under the coffee dispenser and filled it all the way. From the 11-ounce thermos, she then filled up the 7-ounce Thermos and poured the remaining 4 ounces into the 9-ounce Thermos. It looked like this:

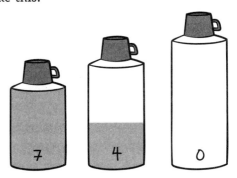

Next, Lori-Beth transferred the coffee from the 7-ounce Thermos into the empty 11-ounce thermos. She then held the 11-ouncer under the dispenser and filled it the rest of the way. And from the 11-ouncer, she filled up the 9-ouncer (it already had 4 ounces in it, so Lori-Beth was able to pour only 5 more ounces in it). The remaining 6 ounces she poured into the 7-ouncer. The Thermoses now held the following:

Finally, Lori-Beth poured the 9-ouncer into the 11-ounce Thermos. She then held the 11-ouncer under the dispenser to fill it.

All Lori-Beth had to do now was fill the 7-ouncer from the 11-ouncer, leaving *exactly* 10 ounces in the 11-ounce Thermos. Mission accomplished:

The students were stunned, as they saw the teacher's pet once again show up everyone in the class. They all waited to hear Mrs. Cook sing Lori-Beth's praises and give her extra credit, but instead they heard her say, "Are you out of your mind, young lady?"

Mrs. Cook's tone wiped Lori-Beth's smirk off her face instantly. "What? What did I do wrong?" asked Lori-Beth.

Mrs. Cook picked up the 7-ounce Thermos and said, "This is what you did wrong. What am I supposed to do with the extra 7 ounces of coffee? I can't pour it back into the dispenser.

It's wasted." And then Mrs. Cook poured the 7 ounces into the sink. "I hate wasting coffee," she snapped. "Now perhaps one of you can come up with another solution that isn't so wasteful."

Lori-Beth slunk back to her seat with her head down and her ego bruised severely. She sat down and picked up her pencil to try again. Before she could collect her thoughts, a hand shot up from the back of the room. "Yes, Wilson? Where's the fire?" asked Mrs. Cook. The class began to chuckle.

In the last seat in the last row by the window sat Wilson Woodrow. With inch-thick glasses, curly red hair, and one ear considerably larger than the other, Wilson always felt self-conscious. Since the beginning of the year, he had raised his hand just one other time in Mrs. Cook's class, and that was only to alert the teacher that he had accidentally started a small fire in his book bag. "No fire, Mrs. Cook. But I think I found a way to get 10 ounces without wasting so much."

Mrs. Cook asked him to go to the coffee dispenser and demonstrate his method. Just as Lori-Beth did, Wilson lined up the 7-ounce, 9-ounce, and 11-ounce Thermoses side by side. He then filled up the 7-ouncer and the 9-ouncer. Next, he poured the contents from the 9-ouncer into the 11-ouncer:

Wilson filled up the 11-ouncer from the 7-ouncer (leaving 5 ounces in the 7-ouncer). He then poured the remaining 5 ounces into the 9-ouncer:

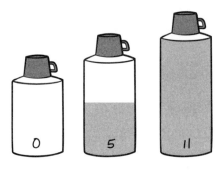

From the 11-ouncer, he filled up the 7-ouncer, leaving 4 ounces in the 11-ouncer:

Then from the 7-ouncer, he filled up the 9-ouncer, leaving 3 ounces in the 7-ouncer:

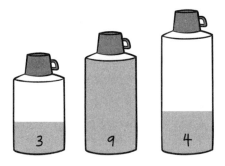

Wilson next did something that caused the class to gasp and made Mrs. Cook bite her lower lip. He emptied the 4 ounces in the 11-ounce Thermos down the sink. "Don't worry, it's only 4

ounces," said Wilson. He then transferred the 3 ounces from the 7-ouncer to the 11-ouncer:

Wilson picked up the full 9-ouncer and poured it into the 7-ouncer, leaving:

As a last step, Wilson poured the 7 ounces from the 7-ouncer into the 3 ounces in the 11-ouncer, leaving 10 ounces exactly.

The class was silent as Mrs. Cook stared at the Thermoses, shaking her head. She picked up the 9-ouncer and poured the remaining 2 ounces down the drain. "You wasted 6 ounces, Wilson, better than Lori-Beth, but still not good enough."

Wilson, about to return to his seat, noticed the paper he had used for his calculations was too close to the coffee machine and had begun to smoke. Within seconds it burst into flames. Mrs. Cook picked up the 11-ouncer, and after a brief moral struggle, doused the fire with the coffee. She then turned to her class and said:

"Can anyone find a way to give me exactly 10 ounces while wasting less than 6 ounces?" *(Solution on page 85.)*

6. The Boiler Room

Vice Principal Magnesium was in the boiler room talking to the school's custodian, Mr. Pock. There was a foul smell in the air, and the hum of the equipment made it difficult to have a conversation. The vice principal was afraid to breathe in the fumes from the boilers, so he held a handkerchief over his mouth. Mr. Pock did not share the VP's concerns, as he munched happily on a tuna-salad sandwich.

"I still don't understand why," said Mr. Magnesium. "It doesn't make sense to me."

"Well, it made perfect sense to me," said the custodian. "Would you like some tuna salad?" he asked, offering the other half of his sandwich.

"No thank you. I've already eaten," mumbled VP Magnesium into his handkerchief. "Then maybe you can explain it to me in words I can understand. Why are the switches that control the lights in my office located the boiler room?"

"Well," said Mr. Pock, as he took another bite of his sandwich, "you see, way, way back, this school wasn't this school at all. Well, it was this school, but not this school as it is today. Ya follow?"

Mr. Magnesium didn't have the faintest idea what the custodian was saying. He breathed deeply into his handkerchief, thinking that it was somehow blocking the soot from the boilers from entering his lungs. "No, I don't follow. What are you talking about?"

Mr. Pock looked at the VP and said, "Forty years ago, when I first started here as the custodian, I was in charge of turning on the lights at the beginning of the day and turning off the lights at the end of the day. Well, even though I was a much younger man then, it was still quite a job to run all over the school turning on and off all the lights in the building. So I decided to rewire the entire school and put all the light switches in the boiler room. This way I could turn the lights on and off in a matter of seconds."

"But that's insane!" the vice principal said with disbelief.

"Oh?" said the custodian. "Is it insane or is it an act of janitorial genius?"

"Janitorial genius?" asked the VP.

"Yes," said Mr. Pock. "Janitorial genius . . . clever custodianism . . . maintenance mastery. I saved quite a bit of time by putting the switches in the boiler room. Of course, since then I've rewired most of the classrooms and offices. I haven't gotten around to yours yet though."

"Oh that's just great," said Mr. Magnesium. "Well, you forgot to turn the lights on in my office today. But I want you to turn on only the two lights in the back. You see, I rearranged my office yesterday, and the light bulb at the front of the room shines directly on top of my head. It feels like it's blinding me."

"Hmm, well that is a problem," sympathized Mr. Pock.

The two men walked over to the control panel and found the switches for Mr. Magnesium's office—room #306. There were three light switches, but none of them were labeled. Mr. Pock stared at the panel for a full minute, trying to figure out which switch controlled which light bulb. "Well, isn't that the darnedest thing. Would you believe that I can't tell which switch controls what?"

"Oh yes. I most certainly would believe that," said Vice Principal Magnesium. "So how are we going to figure out which switch is which?"

Again the two men thought in silence. Mr. Magnesium breathed in and out carefully through his handkerchief, while Mr. Pock stuffed a giant bite of his tuna-salad sandwich into his mouth. Upon swallowing, Mr. Pock said, "I got it! Here's what we'll do. There are three lights and three light switches. We can turn on the first and second switches and then run upstairs to see which two lights are on. After that, we can run back down and turn off switches 1 and 2, but then turn on switches 1 and 3. We can run upstairs again and see which lights are on. And then we can run downstairs, this time turning on lights 2 and 3. Then we can add up all the times each light was on, multiply that by the amount of times each light was off, and divide the total by 9."

"Hold it, hold it! I've heard enough of your janitorial gibberish," said VP Magnesium. "I'm exhausted just listening to you. I think that I have a much better plan that involves us walking up to my office only one time."

Mr. Pock couldn't help but laugh. "Maybe you should stick to education and let me worry about lights, Mr. Magnesium. It's not possible to figure out which switch controls which light bulb with only one trip upstairs."

Who was right? With three light bulbs and three switches, is it possible to determine which switch controls which light bulb with only one trip up to Mr. Magnesium's office? (*Solution on page 88.*)

7. Oh Boy!

Principal Marshall waited in his office for the arrival of Miss Stewart, whom he had summoned over the intercom a short while earlier. He had just taken an aspirin, because he knew from past experience that talking with Miss Stewart for more than five minutes gave him a pounding headache. Today would be no exception.

A moment later, there was a faint tapping on his door. The principal called out, "Come in!" After several seconds of silence, he then heard the same faint tapping at the door. Again he said, "Come in!" He waited several more seconds and still nothing happened. When the principal heard the tapping a third time, he decided to get up and open the door.

When he did, he saw Miss Stewart standing there. "Didn't you hear me say 'Come in?'"

"Yes," replied Miss Stewart.

"Then why didn't you come in?"

"I wasn't sure you were talking to me."

"I only have one door and you were knocking on it. Who else could I possibly have been talking to?"

Miss Stewart reflected and said, "Maybe someone was at the window."

Mr. Marshall silently hoped that the aspirin would start to kick in soon. When he asked Miss Stewart to take a seat, he made sure to look directly at her and use her name, so that she wouldn't think he was talking to someone outside the room, on the telephone, out the window, or hiding behind the plant. Once the teacher sat down, Mr. Marshall got down to business.

"Miss Stewart," he began, "once again, I must talk to you about the same problem that we've been having since the beginning of the school year. It is very frustrating talking about this with you over and over again."

"We can talk about something else if you like, Mr. Marshall," said the clueless teacher.

"No, no, that's not the point. You see, I've been getting more complaints from parents about your classes."

Miss Stewart was very sensitive, and the principal's comments had noticeably disturbed her. "I don't understand. What are they complaining about?"

"The same thing they always complain about: your lessons." Principal Marshall knew he would regret asking his next question, but he did so anyway. "Let me ask you something, Miss Stewart. What have you been teaching your eighth-grade social studies class the past couple of weeks?"

She thought for a moment and replied, "Let's see. This week they're learning how to plan a fabulous party, last week I taught them the proper way to introduce themselves, the week before they learned how to become popular. . . ."

Mr. Marshall put up his hand. "I've heard enough. You don't seem to understand what social studies is all about."

"Of course I do," retorted the young teacher. "They are studying how to be more social. Being popular and friendly are very important social studies. And what could be more social than planning a fabulous party?"

"No! Social studies is not about being 'social,' Miss Stewart. It's about social topics, such as current events or history or politics or the government."

"I don't think that's right. If what you're saying is true, Mr. Marshall, then why don't they call it history studies or current event studies or boring studies? They call it social studies for a reason, Mr. Marshall."

The principal was at his wits' end. "No, Miss Stewart . . . Oh never mind." He put his face in his hands and sighed heavily.

Miss Stewart saw that the principal was under a lot of pressure. "Cheer up, Mr. Marshall. You'll feel a lot better after you catch that boy and girl who stole the tests."

"Yes, maybe you're right. I've been so worried about . . ." Mr. Marshall stopped mid-sentence and stared at the teacher. He said, "Wait a second. You said 'that boy and girl who stole the tests.' What makes you think it was a boy and a girl?"

Miss Stewart thought for a moment and then said, "Well, didn't the note you received say that one of them hid the tests in the boys' locker room while changing for gym?"

"Yes, I suppose it did say that," said the principal.

"Well, unless the girls are allowed to change in the boys' locker room, I think we can say that one of the students is a boy," said the teacher.

The principal nodded in agreement. "Yes, quite right, Miss Stewart, quite right. That explains the boy, but you said it would be a boy and a girl. Isn't it possible that they are both boys?"

"Yes, it's possible, but not very likely, Mr. Marshall."

"Not likely? But why not?" asked the principal.

"Simple mathematics," said Miss Stewart. "Whenever you have two children, one has to be older than the other. Isn't that right, Mr. Marshall?"

The principal thought about it and said, "Yes, I suppose that one will always be older, even if it's only by a day or an hour."

"Exactly," said the teacher. "So if we have two students and one is older than the other, then we have four possible combinations." She then took a pen and a piece of paper from Mr. Marshall's desk and wrote the following:

The older student is a boy and the younger student is a boy.   Boy - Boy

The older student is a boy and the younger student is a girl.   Boy - Girl

The older student is a girl and the younger student is a boy.   Girl - Boy

The older student is a girl and the younger student is a girl.   Girl - Girl

Miss Stewart continued: "But we know that one of the students has to be a boy, so we can eliminate #4, since that's girl-girl." She then took a pen and drew a line through #4. "That means we are left with three possibilities."

The older Student is
a boy and the younger   Boy - Boy
student is a boy.

The older student is
a boy and the younger   Boy - Girl
student is a girl.

The older Student is
a girl and the younger   Girl - Boy
Student is a boy.

~~The older student is
a girl and the younger   Girl - Girl
student is a girl.~~

"As you can see, the second student is a boy in only one of the remaining possibilities. In the other two possibilities, the other student is a girl. Therefore, there is a 2-out-of-3 chance—or two-thirds—that the students who stole the tests are one boy and one girl."

Principal Marshall's head was spinning in disbelief over Miss Stewart's sudden burst of intelligence. But after thinking about it for a moment, he said, "No, Miss Stewart, that's utter nonsense. The only thing that you have proven is that you have an active imagination. You may return to your class now."

Miss Stewart said, "Well, if you say so, Mr. Marshall." She then got up and proceeded to walk into the principal's closet. After several minutes, she came out and left through the door.

Was Miss Stewart right? Knowing that one student is a boy, what is the probability that the other student is a girl? (*Solution on page 88.*)

8. The Class List

Principal Marshall stormed out of his office with a severe headache. His long strides and sour expression told all those in his path to keep out of the way. When he reached Mr. Magnesium's office, he was more than a bit surprised to see the vice principal standing on his desk with his hand around a light bulb. The custodian, Mr. Pock, was standing by the desk taking notes.

"What in blazes is going on in here?" asked the principal.

Mr. Pock approached the principal and said, "It's nothing to worry about, Principal Marshall. Mr. Magnesium is just feeling the light bulb."

"Why is he doing that?" inquired Mr. Marshall, rather impatiently. "And why does it smell like tuna salad in here?"

"Would you like the long version or the short version?" asked the custodian.

Mr. Marshall thought about it and decided he didn't want to hear either version. "Never mind. I have something much more important to discuss." Mr. Magnesium had gotten down from his desk. The principal walked over to him and said, "How is it going with the investigation?"

"Very well," said the vice principal. "I went to the computer lab and checked the system logs for the past few days. I discovered that the midterm exams were last accessed yesterday morning at 10:13 from one of the computers in the lab. Whoever opened the file also printed it."

"I see!" exclaimed the principal. "So all we have to do is to look at the attendance records in the computer lab and we will know exactly who was there when the tests were printed."

"My thoughts exactly," said VP Magnesium. He reached into his desk drawer and grabbed a manila envelope. He opened the envelope and pulled out a sheet of paper. "I already checked the attendance records. On this paper is a list of students who were in the computer lab at the time of the theft."

"Excellent work," said the principal. "But there's something that I don't understand. I thought that the tests were protected by a security system on the computer. How did a student crack the code?"

The vice principal replied, "I'm not sure. But I spoke to the school programmer, who told me that hacking this system would not be easy. Only a student with an A in computers would have any chance of getting to those tests."

"So we had better check the grade book to see which one of these students had an A."

"No need," said Mr. Magnesium. "I already looked up the files and retrieved the grades. Here is the class list for the computer lab. Next to each name is the grade in computers." He handed the principal the class list and sat down.

Principal Marshall took the paper and studied each name and grade. The list was as follows:

CLASS LIST

Rudy Wichter: A

Fran Doyle: B

Alex Silvers: C

Ashleigh Ray: C

Wilson Woodrow: A

Lori-Beth Sugarman: A

Hy November: B

After studying the names, he said, "So we've narrowed it down to eight suspects. And since the note indicated that there were two students involved in the theft, all we have to do is eliminate six names from this list . . . ."

Mr. Pock interrupted the principal's train of thought and said, "Excuse me, Mr. Marshall. I may not be much of a detective, but there are some things I know and some things I don't know. And I know this: The only way you are going to catch your thieves is if you look at them in pairs instead of as individuals."

The principal didn't like what he was hearing. "Mr. Pock," he said, "I am a busy man. I don't have time to sit here and analyze every possible pair of students. Do you have any idea how many pairs that would be? We have 8 suspects, so 8 times 8 makes 64 pairs. That would take all day!"

Mr. Magnesium couldn't keep himself from chuckling. "No," he said as he tried unsuccessfully to quell his laughter. "That isn't how you figure out pairings. You aren't supposed to multiply 8 students by 8 students." He snorted in delight. "Since we're looking for pairs, you're supposed to multiple 8 students by 2. This means that there are only 16 possible pairs."

The principal didn't like being proven wrong, and he especially didn't like being laughed at. Just as he was about to bark at his vice principal, Mr. Pock stepped in. "Well, I also know something else: Neither number is correct. It's more than 16 pairs but a lot less than 64."

Was Mr. Pock right? How many separate pairs can be made with 8 students? (Solution on page 89.)

9. B or Better

The next day, Rodman made it to school on time. He was still not sure where all of his classes were, but he found his Advanced Placement or AP English class without the help of Mr. Pock.

Mrs. Sophie Turkus, the school's top English teacher, was famous throughout the district for her unyielding strictness when it came to the rules of the English language. As a grammar expert and a stickler for details, she did not tolerate the improper use of words or errors in punctuation. Her students quickly learned to mend their split infinitives, curb their dangling participles, and calibrate their subject-verb agreements with precision.

She was most critical of her AP students. This select group of four students (now five, with the addition of Rodman) was her pride and joy. Each year, she hand-picked the brightest and most promising students for her AP class. She then molded them into highly skilled grammarians and writers, whom she often referred to as her "English Enigmas." Although all of the teachers found this nickname very impressive, it also earned her students frequent beatings from the school bullies. Despite that, every year her students received A's on all of her exams.

This school year was different. Her students were undeniably bright, but they weren't meeting Mrs. Turkus's tough standards. Since September, she had grown progressively more dissatisfied with the performance of her pupils. Even though the school year was almost halfway through, she decided that she had to make a stand and show the school that *Mrs. Turkus refuses to accept "good enough."* After all, she had a reputation to maintain.

The bell was about to ring for second period, as Mrs. Turkus's students filed into her class. Having made up her mind to take action, the teacher felt a welcomed sense of relief. When the five students had assembled, Mrs. Turkus stood and cleared her throat.

"Each time I graded your tests and homework this year," she said, "I was faced with appalling grammar: run-on sentences, misplaced modifiers, ambiguous pronouns. It was heartbreaking. I kept hoping that your poor performance was temporary, but it persisted month after month. There were times when I found myself wondering if you even knew the difference between a gerund and an adjective participle! That's how shaken up you've gotten me."

The students looked at each other in bewilderment, not fully understanding what the teacher was saying, but at the same time sensing that something troubling was about to happen.

She continued: "Some of you have met expectations, while others have severely disappointed me. So, I have decided that the poorer performers in the class will have to be removed from Advanced Placement and sent back to General English with the rest of the students."

This news was not welcomed by the class. No student wanted to walk into a new class halfway through the year.

Mrs. Turkus finished her diatribe: "So, those of you who do not have at least a B average in this class are to report to Mr. Weldon's English class for the remainder of the school year. And I will tell you this: At least one of you did not make the grade."

The students were confused, because they were unsure of what their grades actually were. Do I have at least a B average? each student wondered. Even Rodman, who had taken only a placement test before enrolling in the school, was clueless about his grade.

Mrs. Turkus walked around the class handing out envelopes. When each student had one, she said, "I know that all of you must be wondering what your grades are. Look inside your envelope and you will see the class grades written on an index card."

The five AP students sat trembling in their seats, terrified to look inside for fear of discovering that they didn't make the grade. But when they finally mustered the courage to open their envelopes, they found something completely unexpected.

The class remained silent for several minutes, as the students studied the grades. Finally, Fran raised her hand and asked what each of her classmates was thinking. "Mrs. Turkus? The index card you gave me has everyone else's grades in the class—but mine!"

Shouts of "Me too!" and "Same with me!" filled the classroom. Mrs. Turkus put her hand up to quiet down the class. "Yes, I am aware of what is on your index cards. I wrote them. You can each see your classmates' grades, but none of you can see your own grade."

This really perplexed the students. Fran spoke up once again. "Mrs. Turkus? What good is knowing everyone else's grade? We need to know our *own* grades to figure out whether or not we're still in your class."

Mrs. Turkus had anticipated the question. "You have all the information to help you figure out what you want to know. Oh, and you're not allowed to ask your classmates what your grade is. You have to figure it out on your own."

The class was utterly confused. Mrs. Turkus continued: "As soon as you realize that you have less than a B average, stop coming to this class and report directly to Mr. Weldon's English class the following day. You can keep coming here each day until it is logically possible to realize that you didn't make the grade."

"Mrs. Turkus?" asked Fran. "Wouldn't it be easier to tell us who has to leave?"

"Easier, yes, but not as challenging. This is the Advanced Placement class. I think you'll have no trouble determining if you should stay or go. Rodman, since you're new, we will use your grade on the placement test as your class grade. And one more thing: If you each figure out who stays and who goes in the least amount of time possible, I will raise each of your averages by 10 points."

Fran: A
Gordon: B
Rodman: B
Peter: C
Gilbert: C

The class sat in silence for the next 20 minutes, trying to devise a way to determine their own grades. They pondered their clues and conditions:

- They each saw their classmates' grades, but not their own.

- They can't ask their classmates what their grades are.

- At least one student fell below a B.

Students will continue to report to Mrs. Turkus's class. However, once a student realizes that his or her grade is below a B, the student will report to Mr. Weldon's class the following day.

How did they figure this out? How many days did it take Peter and Gilbert to realize they didn't make the grade? (*Solution on page 89.*)

10. The Birthday Miracle

"It's a miracle, I tell you! There's no other explanation. I've never seen anything like it. Just think of the odds! It's got to be one in a million. One in a billion! It must be a sign—a sign that I'm destined to get back on television!"

The students sat in their chairs, staring at their ranting teacher in bewilderment. They were somewhat used to the bizarre behavior of their teacher, Morey Holland, but this time he appeared to have lost it for good. He always talked about how one day he would return to his former glory days and be on another sit-com. And now, because of the "miracle," he was convinced that it would happen soon. Morey saw the perplexed looks on the faces of his students. He said, "What's the matter with you people? Can't you see the miracle that just occurred?"

Apparently, the students did not note anything particularly remarkable. Before Morey Holland arrived, the students were having a small birthday celebration for Jan Rosen, a seventh-grader who recently turned 13. As soon as Morey walked into the classroom and realized what was happening, he started zig-zagging through the rows of chairs, yanking at his remaining hair and raving about miracles and birthdays and signs from the gods.

Molly Peltin—a dark-haired, green-eyed, outspoken student who was president of her seventh-grade class—raised her hand and said, "Excuse me, Mr. Holland, but what's so miraculous about Jan having a birthday? I think that she has one every year." Molly had a reputation for being a smart-aleck who some-times didn't know when to stop. Now was one of those times. She continued: "In fact, most of us have birthdays. I, myself, had one a few weeks ago. It happens."

"Yes, yes, of course it happens," replied the excited TV-star-turned-teacher. "I'm not saying that Jan's birthday is the miracle. It's the fact that her birthday is *today* that makes it so remarkable."

"Why is that?" asked Molly.

Morey Holland looked Molly in the eyes and said in a dramatic tone, "Because today is my birthday too!" There was silence in the room. The students couldn't have been more unimpressed. Morey saw the looks of utter boredom in the faces of the students. "Don't you get it? Don't you think it's a miracle?"

Molly responded, "A miracle? Hardly. A miracle would be something like . . . like Jan growing an eyeball on her tongue, or the school lifting off the ground and  floating in the sky, or you ever getting back on television. Those would be miracles. I'm afraid that you sharing a birthday with Jan doesn't make it a miracle."

"Oh no?" asked the teacher in disbelief. "Then what would you call it?"

Molly said, "I don't know. A coincidence maybe, and not a very big one at that."

"Oh, young lady, you are sadly, sadly mistaken. You see,

there are many days in the year—hundreds of them!"

"Three hundred and sixty-five," said Molly.

"Yes, something like that," Morey responded. "The chances of the two of us sharing a birthday are astronomical! Never in my wildest dreams would I have imagined something as bizarre as this. It's a miracle, I tell you. A pure miracle! It's the kind of thing that can get me out of this small-time teaching gig and back on a sit-com. The newspapers eat this stuff up."

"I hate to burst your bubble," said Molly. "But it's not so unusual for two people in the same class to share a birthday."

"You're crazy! There are only 22 kids in this class. Counting me, that's 23 people. You said yourself that there are three hundred and fifty something days in a year . . ."

"Three hundred and sixty-five," interrupted Molly.

"Yeah, whatever," continued Morey. "That means the odds are something like 365 to 22. A miracle!"

Who's right, Molly or Morey? With 23 people in the class, is it likely that two people (any two people) would share a birthday? What is the minimum number of people needed in a group to make it likely that two people (any two) share a birthday? (*Solution on page 91.*)

11. The Missing Dollar

It was his second day of school, and Rodman was still having a hard time finding his way to his classes. Once again, he was very late for his next period—lunch. He had located the cafeteria the day before, but could not remember the correct route. By the time he arrived, the room was bustling with students who were already in the middle of their lunches and loudly chatting away. He entered the hot-lunch line and had his tray filled with the day's special: soggy meatloaf, a dried-out potato, and a steaming orange blob that he assumed to be some sort of vegetable.

Rodman walked around the lunchroom searching for an empty seat. He felt awkward as he carried his tray further and further into the cafeteria. He was hoping to locate a quiet spot at the end of a table where he could just sit and eat his lunch in peace. Even though he had attended many schools, he was never very good at introducing himself and making new friends. Unfortunately for Rodman, all of the end seats were already taken, and he was not about to insert himself in the middle of a group of strangers while they were having a conversation.

Rodman looked ahead to his left and saw a table mobbed by students. As he got nearer, he noticed that most of the activity was taking place around one girl: Ashleigh Ray. When Rodman saw her, his muscles instinctively tightened and he held his breath in sheer panic. He made eye contact with her for a split second, scrunched his face into an embarrassing position, and put on a forced, awkward smile. As he walked past the table, he made a mental note to give himself a good kick later.

Finally, Rodman saw a table way at the back of the room that appeared to be empty. He started walking faster, grateful that he would not have to eat standing up in some corner. As he got closer to the table, he saw that two kids were sitting there. One was a boy with curly red hair, thick glasses, and uneven ears. Had Rodman made it to Mrs. Cook's math class the day before, he would have recognized him as Wilson Woodrow, the math whiz who had helped figure out how to give Mrs. Cook exactly 10 ounces of coffee. Across from Wilson sat Hy November, a plump, buck-toothed student with chapped lips and large nostrils. Wilson and Hy shared a common interest in chess and a common dislike for popular students, especially every member of the school's sports teams.

Rodman quietly sat down next to Wilson and began to eat his meatloaf, trying his best to mind his own business. At least by sitting at this table, Rodman wouldn't have to get nervous around girls, as Wilson never spoke to any. Wilson was a girl anti-magnet.

Rodman didn't intend to eavesdrop on the conversation between Wilson and Hy, but they were talking so loudly he had no choice. Hy was in the middle of telling a story:

"No, I swear, there was a missing dollar!"

"What do you mean it was missing?" asked Wilson.

"It was missing, it was gone, it somehow disappeared!" cried Hy.

Wilson gestured for Hy to slow down. "Okay, don't get so excited. You're going to have to take it easy and start from the beginning."

Hy took a deep breath and collected his thoughts. "Okay, fine. Here's what happened: Yesterday after school, my mother gave me 20 dollars to buy a new food bowl for our cat, Merky. So I walked down to the pet store and found one. But when I went to pay for the bowl, I saw that it cost only 15 dollars. So the saleslady gave me 5 dollars back."

"So," said Wilson, "the bowl was 15 dollars, and you got 5 dollars change—15 and 5 is 20. There is no missing dollar."

Rodman continued to eat his meatloaf, growing more and more interested in Hy's story. He was curious about the missing dollar that the buck-toothed kid was talking about. Rodman pretended not to listen, as he forced himself to swallow the steaming orange mush.

"Well, you didn't let me finish my story," said Hy. "You see, on the way home, I was passing Kelly's Candy Corner, and I thought I would take a little peek inside. Once I was in the store, I couldn't help but buy a couple of candy bars for 2 dollars."

"So then you had 3 dollars left," noted Wilson.

"Exactly," replied Hy. "I had 3 dollars left. So when I got home, I gave my mom Merky's bowl and the 3 dollars' change. She said, 'Oh, I see that the bowl only cost 17 dollars.' I said, 'Yeah, it cost 17 dollars.'"

"You didn't tell her about the candy bars?" inquired Wilson.

Hy said, "Well, no. I sort of forgot about that part. Besides, she seemed happy that she only had to pay 17 dollars for the bowl instead of 20."

"Okay, but I still don't see the missing dollar you are talking about," said Wilson.

"You don't? But it's so obvious!" insisted Hy. "Look, altogether how much money did my mom spend?"

Wilson thought for a moment and said, "Well, she gave you 20 dollars, and she got back 3 dollars' change. So that means she spent a total of 17 dollars."

"Yes, 17 dollars. And how much did my candy bars cost?"

"Your candy bars cost 2 dollars," said Wilson.

Hy looked his friend in the eye and said, "Exactly. My mom spent 17 dollars and I spent 2 dollars. And 17 + 2 is only 19. My mom gave me 20 dollars!"

The two boys looked at each other and said in unison, "Where's the missing dollar?"

Rodman shook his head silently, not quite believing what he was hearing. Although he didn't make it a habit of butting into other people's conversations, he couldn't help himself this time. He took one more forkful of the orange mush, swallowed hard, and said, "Excuse me, I know that this is none of my business, but I think I can help you figure out what happened to the missing dollar."

What was Rodman's explanation? (*Solution on page 94.*)

12. Three Amigos, a Janitor, and an Elevator

Rudy Wichter stuck his head outside of Mr. Raccoon's science room. He looked to his left down the hallway and saw no one. He turned his head to the right and saw no one. The coast was clear. He stepped into the hallway and motioned for the others to join him. A few seconds later, Alex Silvers emerged from the room, followed closely by their teacher, Mr. Raccoon. The teacher was hunched over, carrying the heavy safe that they had been arguing over the day before. To avoid arousing anyone's suspicions, they had cleverly covered the safe with a shiny purple cloth.

The three of them (who Rodman called the "Three Amigos") were on the move. They had decided it was too dangerous to keep the safe in the classroom, so they made a plan to hide it in the woods behind the school. They had taken Rodman's advice and put three locks on the safe. Each of the Amigos had two keys. This way any two of them could open the safe together, but none of them could open it alone.

They hustled down the hallway, the teacher hugging the safe in his arms. With each new step, Mr. Raccoon could feel the 50-pound safe slowly slipping out of his straining fingers. He sure could use some help, but he didn't trust the students to have possession of the safe, not even for a minute. The three of them moved quickly toward the staircase—just a short 100 feet from the classroom. On the way, they passed the service elevator, which, as everyone knew, was strictly off-limits to students and faculty. When they reached the end of the hall, they were severely disappointed to find that the stairway door was locked, with a sign on the window that said "Closed for repairs. Use other staircase."

They looked at each other with despair. The other staircase was clear across the school, and, although classes were in session, they would be taking a huge risk of being seen if they had to haul the safe that far—despite their clever purple camouflage. Besides, the weight of the safe was threatening to pull Mr. Raccoon's arms right out of their sockets. All at once, the three of them turned to look at the service elevator. They knew that they would be in a world of trouble if they were caught using the elevator, but right now it seemed to be the best solution.

Mr. Raccoon led the group toward the elevator, as he used almost all of his remaining strength to muscle the safe along. Alex pressed the button, and they waited for it to arrive from the boiler room. When the elevator came to a stop, the doors opened and the Three Amigos barged ahead to get inside, almost slamming into Mr. Pock and his maintenance cart.

The custodian let out a yelp, as he saw the teacher and two students come charging at him. "Slow down! You almost ran me over! Are you people crazy? You're not allowed in here!"

The Three Amigos stopped in their tracks before stepping into the elevator. Rudy started pleading with Mr. Pock. "No, you don't understand. You have to let us use the elevator. It's an emergency!"

"An emergency? I don't understand what's so urgent that you can't take the stairs down. No one but me is allowed on this elevator," said Mr. Pock.

Upon hearing that, Mr. Raccoon lost feeling in his right arm. The weight of the safe was too much to take, and it was making him grow numb. And his face was starting to turn red. "What is going on here?" Mr. Pock said, sensing that something wasn't right.

"Oh, nothing," said Mr. Raccoon, with sweat dripping down his temples. "Nothing at all going on. Just a little science experiment, that's all."

"Is that a fact?" said Mr. Pock. "As it happens, I am a big fan of science. Did I ever tell you that my grandfather used to conduct experiments with stale cheese? That's science, no?"

They didn't quite know how to respond to that. The more Mr. Pock droned on, the closer Mr. Raccoon came to passing out. Finally, he blurted out, "Please, Mr. Pock, in the name of science, let us take the service elevator!"

Mr. Pock stroked his chin and said, "Well, I suppose that I could make an exception—in the name of science, that is. But the elevator is not very safe, and I will have to escort you down. The problem is that my maintenance cart takes up most of the room, which means that only one of you can fit in the elevator with me at a time."

This presented an immediate dilemma for the Three Amigos. It occurred to them that if they went down one at a time, then at some point two of them would be alone with the safe, and neither of them would agree to this. They began to bicker back and forth, arguing about who would be the last one down.

"Okay, who's first?" asked the janitor.

The three of them couldn't agree on the order they would go down. In short, this was their problem:

- If one of the students went down first, then the other student would remain upstairs with Mr. Raccoon, and the two of them would be able to open the safe without the third one being present.

Mr. Raccoon could go down first, since he wouldn't be able to open the safe by himself. But then, which student would go down second? The student who was left behind would worry that the other two were opening the safe without him.

The three of them could not seem to find a solution. Every idea they suggested would at some point leave two of them alone with the safe. When they realized they could not find an answer, they began arguing again.

After listening to them bicker back and forth for a few minutes, Mr. Pock had heard enough. "Hold on there! Let me see if I've got this straight," he said. "The three of you need to get to the first floor, is that right?"

They nodded in agreement.

"And for some reason you can't let two of you be alone with the heavy purple science experiment. And Mr. Raccoon has to carry it at all times. Is that right?"

Again, the three nodded yes.

The janitor scratched his forehead and squinted his eyes to help him think better. He then began drawing imaginary mathematical equations in the air. After a moment, he said, "Well, I may not be a smart teacher like you, Mr. Raccoon, but there are some things I know and some things I don't know. And one thing I do know is that there is a way it can be done."

What was the janitor's idea? How can he get the three of them downstairs by taking them one at a time—without allowing two of them to be alone with the safe? (*Solution on page 94.***)**

13. They're Closing In

For the second time in two days, Principal Marshall called an emergency meeting with his department heads. They were summoned over the loudspeaker to stop what they were doing and report to the faculty conference room immediately. This meant that they had to interrupt their lessons and leave in the middle of class.

Within minutes, the department heads were assembled in the conference room, taking the same seats as the day before, with the exception of Mr. Raccoon, who was noticeably absent. Apparently, he thought that whatever he was doing was more important than Principal Marshall's meeting.

While the department heads waited for the principal to arrive, Morey Holland was relaying his story of the birthday miracle to his colleagues, whose expressions ranged from complete indifference to excruciating boredom. Mrs. Turkus listened intently, only to cringe each time Morey ended a sentence with a preposition.

Mrs. Cook was three sips into her late-late-mid-mid-late-mid-mid-late afternoon cup of coffee, mentally calculating how many more sips of heaven were left in the cup. Miss Stewart occupied herself by thumbing through the latest issue of *Party Planning Magazine*, searching for ideas for her next social studies lesson. Vice Principal Magnesium sat quietly, thinking about rewiring his office.

Without warning, Principal Marshall charged into the room, practically knocking Morey off his chair and severely jeopardizing his chances at ever having matching birthdays with anyone again.

The principal got right down to business. He said, "Because of Mr. Magnesium's hard work, we have been able to narrow down the list of suspects considerably." He then explained to his staff about the computer lab and the eight students who had had the opportunity to print out the tests. He also mentioned that one of the thieves had to have a grade of A in computers. The principal walked to the blackboard and wrote down their names along with their grades in the computer class:

RUDY WICHTER : A
FRAN DOYLE : B
ALEX SILVERS : C
ASHLEIGH RAY : C
WILSON WOODROW : A
LORI-BETH SUGARMAN : A
MOLLY PELTIN : A
HY NOVEMBER : B

He said, "We know that two students in this class were involved in the theft. We also know that at least one of the two students is a boy. As Mr. Pock pointed out to me earlier, we have to look at students in pairs instead of individually if we want to figure out who stole the tests. With a total of 8 students as suspects, it is possible to make 28 different pairs. One of these pairs is responsible for the theft." He then handed a chart to everyone present:

Rudy	Rudy	Rudy	Rudy	Rudy	Rudy	Rudy
Fran	Ashleigh	Alex	Wilson	Lori-Beth	Molly	Hy

Fran	Fran	Fran	Fran	Fran	Fran
Ashleigh	Alex	Wilson	Lori-Beth	Molly	Hy

Ashleigh	Ashleigh	Ashleigh	Ashleigh	Ashleigh
Alex	Wilson	Lori-Beth	Molly	Hy

Alex	Alex	Alex	Alex
Wilson	Lori-Beth	Molly	Hy

Wilson	Wilson	Wilson
Lori-Beth	Molly	Hy

Lori-Beth	Lori-Beth
Molly	Hy

Molly
Hy

The room was silent as the staff studied the possible combinations. Finally, Miss Stewart rose and said, "Um, Mr. Marshall? Based on the information you gave us, I think that you can reduce the amount of pairs from 28 to 17."

Everyone looked at Miss Stewart in amazement. They began thinking about the facts that Mr. Marshall had presented, as they studied the list. One by one, they started nodding their heads in agreement, understanding exactly what Miss Stewart was saying.

Just then, the principal's secretary barged into the room. "Mr. Marshall, you're needed down the hall at the service elevator right away. It's urgent."

"None of you leave," ordered Mr. Marshall. "I will be right back." The principal darted out of the room.

Based upon the information Mr. Marshall presented, how can those 28 pairs of suspects be reduced to 17 pairs? (*Solution on page 95.*)

14. To Tell the Truth

As Mr. Pock deposited the Three Amigos on the first floor, he was overwhelmed with a very uneasy feeling. Something didn't seem right, and he was determined to get to the bottom of it. He thought to himself . . . Hmm. That purple thing doesn't look much like a science experiment. And I don't remember my grandfather's cheese looking so heavy.

Mr. Pock decided to investigate further. He said, "I sure would love to get a look at your science experiment."

Mr. Raccoon began to stammer: "Yes, well no, well you see, the thing is, um . . . that's not a very good idea."

"It's just a safe," said Alex.

"A safe?" questioned the custodian. "I thought you said it was a science experiment. What do you mean it's a safe?"

Mr. Raccoon blurted, "No, no, that's not what he said. He didn't say it was *a* safe. He said that it's *not* safe . . . It's not safe to show you the experiment."

This confused Mr. Pock. "Not safe? Why is that?"

"Good question, that's a very good question," said Mr. Raccoon, trying to stall for time. "A good, good, really good question."

"And the answer?" asked Mr. Pock.

"It's not safe because of the . . . um, missing safety factor," said Mr. Raccoon.

"Yes, the factor of missing safety," confirmed Rudy.

Mr. Pock wasn't buying it. He was more suspicious than ever, convinced that they were up to no good. He got on his walkie-talkie and called down to the principal's office.

The Three Amigos tried desperately to talk him out of it, but it was too late. He told the principal's secretary to send Mr. Marshall down to the service elevator right away. Mr. Pock kept a close eye on them, until the principal could be seen turning the corner and walking hurriedly toward the elevator. Mr. Raccoon and the students began to panic.

When Mr. Marshall was within hearing distance, he called out, "What's this about, Mr. Pock? My secretary said it was urgent."

"I thought that you would be interested in seeing a little science experiment, that's all," said Mr. Pock.

"A science experiment?" asked the principal. "Mr. Pock, the last time you called me down to see a science experiment, it took three weeks for us to get the smell of rotten cheese out of the school."

"No, no, it's nothing like that, I can assure you," said the janitor. "This experiment has to do with whatever is hidden under that purple cloth."

"Well, Mr. Raccoon? What's under the cloth?" queried the principal.

"Oh, heh-heh, nothing of interest," said the agitated science teacher. "Just a little experiment we're conducting. I'll be happy to show you when we're finished."

"No, I think you'll show me now," demanded the principal. "Off with the cloth." Mr. Marshall reached out, grabbed a hold of the purple covering, and with one quick yank exposed the safe. At the same time, the weight had become too much to bear, and the safe slipped from Mr. Raccoon's fingers, making a loud thud on the tile floor.

For a moment everyone was silent. Then Mr. Marshall said, "Is that a safe? What on earth are you doing with a safe in the school? It doesn't make sense. What could be so important that you'd have to keep it locked in a . . ."

Just then, Mr. Marshall had a thought. Everything was beginning to crystallize and make perfect sense. It occurred to him that both Rudy and Alex were on the list of students who had been in the computer lab when the tests were stolen. He remembered that Rudy had gotten an A in computers. And he couldn't help but notice that at least one of them was a boy. These boys fit the description of the suspects perfectly. Mr. Marshall's heart began to beat wildly in his chest. He said sternly, "Open that safe this instant!"

The jig was up. The two students were beginning to panic. They fumbled through their pockets, and each pulled out their keys. With shaking hands, they inserted three keys and opened the locks. Principal Marshall's eyes widened, as he anticipated the end of this horrible fiasco. He placed his hand on the safe handle and turned. With one quick motion, he flung the door to the safe open. His jaw dropped and he gasped as he saw what was inside.

The moment the safe was opened, a heap of candy bars poured out into the hallway. The entire contents of the vending machine in the faculty dining room was now lying on the floor in front of the service elevator.

When Mr. Marshall saw that the tests weren't in the safe, he breathed a deep sigh of disappointment. He said, "Well, at least we know who stole the candy from the vending machine. Mr. Pock, exactly what is going on here?"

"Well, the three of them talked me into taking them down the service elevator," said the janitor. "And when they refused to show me what was under the purple cloth, I became very suspicious."

"That's not what happened!" said Rudy. "We were walking down the hall when we saw Mr. Pock come out of the service elevator carrying the safe. We knew he was hiding something, so we stopped him."

"Yeah," joined in Alex. "Then we took the safe away from him and called down to the office."

Principal Marshall didn't believe the students. "That's funny. My secretary said that it was Mr. Pock who called the office on the walkie-talkie."

"I was doing my Mr. Pock impersonation," said Alex.

"You know, boys," said the principal, "stealing is bad enough, but it's the lying that really gets me. I've heard about all I can stand of your outright, brazen lies. So, here's what I'll do: Mr. Raccoon, I'll deal with you later in my office. As for Rudy and Alex, I'll allow you both to determine your own fate."

"What do you mean? " asked the boys.

"What I mean is this: I am going to give you each one chance to tell me the truth. I want you each to make a statement—any statement at all. If that statement is true, you will receive five days of detention. But if it's another lie, I am going to suspend you for five days. Is that understood?"

The boys nodded. "Any statement at all?" asked Rudy. "I can say 'the sky is blue' if I want?"

"Yes, any statement at all," replied the principal. Mr. Marshall looked back and forth from one boy to the other. "Alex, you will go first."

Alex thought carefully. He was terrified of the possibility of being suspended. His parents would ground him forever. He was going to say 'the sky is blue,' but he remembered that it was a little cloudy that day. Instead, he said the one thing that he was 100 percent, completely sure of. He said, "My name is Alex."

"Well done, Alex," said the principal. "You made a smart choice. I am giving you five days of detention starting tomorrow." Alex looked relieved. Principal Marshall now turned his attention to Rudy. "Well, Rudy, it's up to you now. The truth gets you a detention, but a lie will get you suspended. What's it going to be?"

Rudy thought hard for a moment and was suddenly struck with an idea. He then made a statement that left the principal speechless. After hearing it, Mr. Marshall was unable to punish Rudy with detention or suspension. He had no choice but to let him go.

What was Rudy's statement? (*Solution on page 96.*)

15. Inkredible Discovery

By this point, all of the teachers and students were well aware of the stolen exams and were instructed to keep an eye out for clues to their whereabouts. The principal even offered a reward to anyone who had information leading to the discovery of the tests. Most of the school was in a frenzy searching for the exams.

But the midterm exams were the last thing on Rodman's mind. It was his second day in the new school, and all he wanted was to find his way and fit in. The school was large and he still didn't have a good sense of where his classes were, which is why he kept getting lost. And it wasn't entirely his fault. The classrooms were broken up by subject rather than floors and numbers. It usually took the students several days each year to get used to the system.

Rodman was, as usual, late for his next class and found himself wandering aimlessly through the corridors. The bell had rung minutes before, and Rodman was again the only student in the hallway. As he turned a corner, he saw Principal Marshall talking with Mr. Pock and the Three Amigos. Rodman stopped in his tracks and turned around. The last thing he wanted was to have to explain to the school principal why he was late to class.

Rodman wound his way through the halls, up the stairs, around corners, up more stairs, and down more corridors. He found himself in a part of the school where he had not been before. He sensed that he had gone up one floor too many. The classrooms were all locked and dark, and there wasn't a soul around. It felt eerie to be in such a secluded part of the school. Rodman knew he was far from where he should be and tried to trace his path back.

Had he made a left or a right at this corner? He couldn't remember. Rodman decided to make a right, but nothing looked familiar. As he continued walking in isolation, he could hear his footsteps, his breathing, even his heartbeat—which was quickening at the thought of being lost.

He reached a dead end and turned around. As he did, he caught a glimpse of a skinny closet in the corner. It looked like the lock had been broken and bent in. The door was slightly ajar. Unable to quell his curiosity, Rodman walked over to the closet and opened the door. The closet was completely empty, except for three small boxes on the floor. Rodman bent down to examine the boxes more closely. He saw that each box had a label. The first one said PERMANENT INK. Rodman didn't like the sound of that. The label on the second box said DRIED SNAKE POOP. Rodman made a face and fought back the urge to puke. The label on the third box said MIDTERM EXAMS.

When Rodman read the third label, he gasped and did a double-take. He muttered, "Hmm. These must be the tests everyone has been talking about!" He was about to pick up that box, when he saw a note on top. He grabbed it and began reading. It said:

Well, well, well, congratulations on finding the exams. We had a feeling that someone would find them sooner or later. But don't think it's going to be so easy! You see three boxes in front of you.

In one box, there is exploding permanent ink. As soon as you lift the cover off the box, a spring will be activated and bright purple ink will be sprayed for 100 feet. Anyone around will be instantly covered with ink—permanently! It won't come out no matter what you do.

In another box is snake poop. And not just your everyday snake poop either. This stuff was imported from Tanzania, which, as you know, has the smelliest snake poop in the world. If you open that box, another spring will be activated, and everyone will be covered in the stuff instantly. Gross!

In the last box are the midterm exams that we stole. So, congratulations. You have your precious exams back.

Oh, and one more thing. I purposely labeled each box incorrectly. SUCKERS! Good luck in figuring it out! Mwahahahaha.

"*Diabolical!*" Rodman said to himself. He certainly didn't want to risk being stained permanently, and he didn't relish the thought of coming face to face with Tanzanian snake droppings. So he gathered up the boxes, grabbed the note, and started to make his way down the hall. After a few strides, his walk turned into a jog and then an all-out run as he searched for a staircase.

After a minute, Rodman was breathing heavily, but he refused to slow down. He kept turning corners and running at full speed, knowing that eventually he would have to come to a staircase. At the end of the next corridor, he saw the doors leading to the stairs. His heart pounded wildly, as he suspected that he may have found what the entire school was searching for. He raced down the stairs, hoping that Principal Marshall was still in the hallway. When he exited the staircase on the first floor, there was no one in sight. Tightly clutching the boxes, he dashed down the hall to the principal's office.

When he arrived at the outer office, he was breathing so hard that he could barely speak. Approaching the principal's secretary, he uttered: "Mr. . . . Marshall . . . boxes . . . I have . . . tests . . . exploding ink . . . snake poop . . . midterms."

The secretary looked confused. "Young man, you're making no sense at all. You're going to have to calm down and collect your thoughts."

Rodman took a moment to catch his breath. Soon he was able to speak normally. "I think I found something that Mr. Marshall would want to see."

She glanced down at the boxes Rodman was carrying and saw the one labeled SNAKE POOP.

"Is this some kind of joke?" asked the secretary. "Because I can assure you that Mr. Marshall will not be amused. The principal is in an important meeting now and can't be disturbed." She pointed to the door of the faculty conference room.

"But he really needs to see this," pleaded Rodman. "I have to speak to him right away."

"I'm sorry. You will just have to take a seat and wait until his meeting is over," said the secretary.

"Yes, ma'am," replied Rodman.

Rodman was about to sit down, when he suddenly changed his mind. Although he had never gone against a direct order before, he knew that Mr. Marshall would want to see him immediately. So instead of sitting down as he had been told, Rodman breezed past the secretary and headed straight for the faculty conference room. "Hey, you can't go in there!" cried out the secretary. But Rodman completely ignored her, turned the knob, and stepped inside.

He instantly felt overwhelmed, as all heads turned to look in his direction. "What is the meaning of this? What do you think you're doing?" screeched the principal.

Rodman again lost his capacity to speak. He scanned the room and saw that everyone was waiting for an explanation. He opened his mouth, hoping that what he was going to say would somehow make sense: "I found tests and boxes and ink and poop and . . . and . . ."

Once he said the word "tests," the principal walked over and snatched the boxes out of Rodman's hands. He placed them down on the conference table and said, "Oh my, are these the midterm exams?"

Mr. Marshall was about to take the lid off the box marked MIDTERM EXAMS, when Rodman screamed, "*No!*"

The principal hesitated and said, "What do you mean, no? Are these the tests or not?"

Rodman stammered, "Well, yes, er, no. I mean . . . read the note!" He handed the note to the principal, who read it aloud to his staff.

For the next several minutes, Rodman was completely ignored as he listened to the principal and the department heads brainstorm to try to come up with a safe way to get to the tests. "We know that the boxes are all labeled incorrectly, so we can't just open the box that says MIDTERM EXAMS," said the principal. "We could all get sprayed with ink! Since there are three boxes, we only have a 33 percent chance of getting it right on the first try."

They had discussed holding the boxes out the window before opening them, but they didn't want to mark the building with permanent ink. Mr. Magnesium suggested opening the boxes underwater, but that was no guarantee they wouldn't get sprayed. Finally, they decided to play it safe. Rather than take a chance of spraying people with permanent ink, they would take the boxes to the police station where they could be x-rayed.

As they were about to leave the conference room, Rodman spoke up: "Wait, I have an idea." All eyes were back on him. "I think I know a way you can find the tests without worrying about being sprayed with ink."

The principal walked over to Rodman and said, "Well, I'd be very interested in hearing your idea, young man."

What was Rodman's idea? (*Solution on page 96.*)

16. And Then There Were Two

Now that the exams had been recovered, Principal Marshall felt a welcomed sense of relief. Although he was no longer worried about the tests being distributed to the students, he still desperately wanted to find out who was responsible for the theft. His department heads were still assembled in front of him in the faculty conference room. He had decided to let Rodman stay, since he had been so helpful in finding the exams. Mr. Pock and the cleaning crew were also in the room, working hard trying to scrape the Tanzanian snake poop off the walls.

The department heads read the note over and over, finding new clues each time. They examined the class list and discussed each student and pair who remained as suspects. Here is the list of the 17 pairs of students who were still suspects:

Rudy	Rudy	Rudy	Rudy	Rudy	Rudy	Rudy
Fran	Ashleigh	Alex	Wilson	Lori-Beth	Molly	Hy

Fran	Ashleigh	Alex	Alex	Alex
Wilson	Wilson	Wilson	Lori-Beth	Molly

Wilson	Wilson	Wilson	Lori-Beth	Molly
Lori-Beth	Molly	Hy	Hy	Hy

As each new clue emerged, they were able to eliminate suspects from the list until finally there was only one pair left. Can you do the same?

By reading over the note, the list of suspects, and the chapters in which they appear, you will have all the facts needed to crack the case wide open. So, it's up to you! Which two students stole the midterm exams? (*Solution on page 97.*)

17. The Students' Dilemma

At last Principal Marshall was able to solve the case of the stolen exams and identify the two culprits behind the theft. Through a process of elimination, he narrowed down his list of suspects from 28 pairs to only a single pair: Wilson Woodrow and Hy November. Although Mr. Marshall knew beyond a shadow of a doubt that these two students were the thieves, he had no hard evidence, no absolute proof. All he knew was that it had to be them because it couldn't be anyone else. But if he was going to hand out stiff punishments, he needed evidence. Mr. Marshall was determined to get one or both of the students to confess.

The principal summoned the two boys out of their classes to report immediately to his office. When they arrived, they took seats in the outer office by the secretary's desk and began whispering to each other. When Mr. Marshall walked into the room, the students immediately clammed up and looked at the principal defiantly.

Mr. Marshall decided to speak to them separately to see if he could get them to contradict each other's stories. He studied both students, trying to determine who would be the easiest to crack. After much consideration, he pointed at Wilson and ordered him to go to his office. As Wilson rose from his chair, Hy barked at him, "*Remember the pact!*"

Mr. Marshall escorted Wilson into his office and instructed him sit down in the chair opposite his desk. As the principal took his seat behind the desk, the two of them entered into a staring contest. Towering over the student, Mr. Marshall tried to intimidate him with his size and authority, but Wilson would not back down. He stared right back at the principal and refused to flinch.

Principal Marshall realized that this wasn't going to be easy. He stood up and began pacing. After several uncomfortable moments of silence, the principal said, "Tell me, why did you do it?"

Wilson looked at the principal with the most innocent expression he could muster and said, "Why did I do what? I don't know what you're talking about." If Mr. Marshall had even the slightest doubt that Wilson stole the tests, it was completely erased by Wilson's obvious little innocent act, which infuriated the principal even more.

"Why you dirty, lying, no good . . ." Mr. Marshall stopped himself before he said something he would regret. "So, if that's how you want to play," he said, "I can play hardball too, you know. Look, I will be honest with you. I do not have enough evidence to expel you from school for stealing the exams, so I am going to need a confession from either you or Hy."

"A confession? That's a good one!" said Wilson in a mocking tone. "Do you really think one of us would be stupid enough to confess to something we didn't even do? Forget it. We have a pact."

"Oh, you have a pact. I see," said Mr. Marshall, taking his seat again. "Well, I may not have evidence to get you on the stolen tests, but I do have something else." The principal opened a drawer and pulled out a folder. He said, "I have checked Hy's and your attendance records and discovered that the two of you have skipped gym class almost every day for the last three months."

"So, we skipped a few classes, big deal. We hate gym," said Wilson. "That doesn't mean we're going to confess to stealing the exams."

"We will see about that." The principal sat forward, leaning his massive forearms on the desk, and stared at Wilson directly in the eyes. "I am going to give you both two options," he said, "to confess or to remain silent. That means that one of three things can happen.

"If you keep your pact and you both remain silent, I will not have any evidence that you stole the tests. Therefore, I won't be able to throw you out of school. But because I've caught you cutting classes, I can at least give both of you detention for a month.

"If one of you confesses and the other doesn't, then I am going to throw the student who *didn't confess* out of the school permanently. And I am going to reward the student who *did confess* by letting him off the hook completely.

"However, if both of you confess, I won't throw either of you out of school, since you both decided to cooperate. Instead, each of you will have to serve detention until the end of the year. So tell me," added the principal, "do you think your pact is strong enough to withstand that?"

Wilson was not as sure of himself as he had been earlier. He stammered, "Well, yes . . . sort of. Anyway, I'm not going to confess. Neither is Hy. I don't care what you do."

"Is that a fact?" said the principal. "Keep in mind that I will be presenting Hy with the same options. I'm sure you will both realize it's in your best interest to confess. Are you going to take the chance of being thrown out of school permanently? I don't think Hy will."

Wilson remained silent. Mr. Marshall could tell that the student was thinking this over carefully.

Finally, the principal felt as if he had the upper hand. He smiled confidently and said, "I'll give you a few minutes to think this over. In the meantime, I will have a talk with Hy." Mr. Marshall left the room briskly, muttering to himself, "That should get the little thief to spill the beans."

Was Principal Marshall right? Is it likely that one or both students will confess to the crime? (*Solution on page 99.*)

18. Surprise, Surprise!

Woodrow and Hy sat outside the principal's office in awkward silence. They had each privately confessed to Mr. Marshall and were now anxiously awaiting his arrival to hear their punishment. Neither of them knew whether or not the other one had confessed or remained silent.

Mr. Marshall walked in with a broad smile on his face. "Well, boys, thanks so much for your help. Now that I have both of your confessions, I can put an end to this messy affair."

It was then that each student realized he had been double-crossed by the other. Their feelings of guilt were soon replaced by outrage and anger. *"How could you do this to me*?" cried Woodrow. *"You dirty double-crosser*!" answered Hy.

The principal said, "You've both confessed to stealing the midterm exams. So, according to our deal, you will each serve detention until the end of the year."

The punishment hit the students hard, as they wondered how they were going to break the news to their parents. "What day will the detentions begin?" asked Woodrow.

Mr. Marshall said, "I have decided that your detention will begin one day next week. But because you have put me through so much agony, I am not going to tell you what day it is going to be. It will come as a complete surprise to you. One day next week when you come to school, I will tap you on the shoulder and tell you to call your parents. You'll never see it coming." Mr. Marshall wanted to make it as difficult as he could on the students. "You may both report back to your classes now," he said, as he turned and walked back into his office.

The boys couldn't believe how badly they had been tricked by the principal. They sat there wallowing in despair. Suddenly, Wilson was struck with a thought. He said, "Wait a minute! Principal Marshall said that detention will start one day next week but we won't know what day it is going to be. Don't you see what that means? If the day detention starts will come as a surprise, then our detentions can never happen at all!"

Huh? Is Wilson losing his mind or is he onto something? Since Principal Marshall said that the day detentions will start will come as a surprise, is it possible that detentions will never happen? (*Solution on page 101.*)

19. Rodman's Choice

Rodman had found the midterm exams, much to the delight of Mr. Marshall. As promised, the principal was prepared to give Rodman a suitable reward. The midyear assembly was approaching fast, and Principal Marshall planned an elaborate ceremony where he would present Rodman with a plaque and give him an opportunity to earn a substantial reward. But he was going to make Rodman work for it.

On the day of the assembly, the students and teachers gathered in the auditorium class by class. When the entire school was assembled, Principal Marshall walked to the stage and took the microphone. He quieted the room and said:

"As the principal, I believe that I speak on behalf of all of us here at Riddle Middle School when I say that we owe a large debt of gratitude to our newest student—a young man who uncovered a major scandal that would have meant disaster for Riddle. Let's all stand and show our appreciation to the Student of the Year, Mr. Rodman Pilgrim."

The teachers and students stood and filled the auditorium with thunderous applause. Blushing, Rodman waved to the crowd and mouthed a humble "thank you" to those around him. Principal Marshall signaled for Rodman to join him on the stage. Rodman slowly made his way to the front of the room. The principal hushed the crowd and instructed them to sit. He then continued:

"Because of your efforts, Rodman, we are no longer in danger of having the midterm exams distributed to all of the eighth-graders. Not only would that have been disastrous, but quite an embarrassment for our school as well. So I would like to give you something to show my appreciation." The crowd once again applauded generously, eager for Rodman to earn a reward for his good deed.

Principal Marshall handed Rodman a wrapped package and gestured for him to open it. Rodman wiped his sweaty palms on the sides of his pants and then ripped into the wrapping. He revealed a sparkling plaque with an inscription that said *Thank you, Rodman.* Rodman stood there staring at his plaque, completely bewildered.

"I don't mean to sound ungrateful," said Rodman, "but, is this all?"

"Is something wrong?" asked Principal Marshall. "Were you expecting more?"

"Well, sir," began Rodman. "I heard a rumor about some sort of big reward."

"Oh, a reward," said Principal Marshall coyly. He reached into his jacket pocket and produced three envelopes, numbered one, two, and three. He then pinned them to a corkboard so that all in attendance could see them.

The principal said, "Rodman, in one of these envelopes is a check for 1,000 dollars. The other two envelopes only contain pictures of teachers. I am going to give you a choice. You can either keep the plaque or trade it in for the opportunity to pick one of the three envelopes."

This stunned the crowd. Rodman began sweating like a madman. He stared at the plaque, thinking what a great honor it was, but then he would have to pass up a one-out-of-three chance of winning 1,000 dollars.

Gradually, people began shouting out their opinions to Rodman. Once Morey Holland bellowed, "Go for the plaque, you idiot!", the rest of the audience insisted on making their thoughts known. The auditorium filled with a cacophony of voices screaming at Rodman, trying to convince him to gamble for the big money. The only one who remained calm was Mrs. Cook, who stayed in her seat sipping her mid-mid-late-special-occasion-assembly cup of java.

While the audience was on their feet screaming intensely, Rodman scanned the crowd and happened to make eye contact with Ashleigh Ray, the school's head cheerleader. She was smiling at him and holding up an envelope—the very envelope that she had taken from him when they first met. Instantly, Rodman blurted out, "Okay, okay. I will go for the envelope!" The audience erupted in applause, hooting and hollering.

Before Rodman knew what was happening, Principal Marshall had snatched the plaque out of his hands. "Now, Rodman, think carefully. If you select the correct envelope, you will win 1,000 dollars. But if you pick one of the wrong envelopes, you will go home with a picture of one of your teachers. And, to make sure you have every possible benefit, I will do something helpful: After you have made your selection, I will remove one of the wrong envelopes and then give you an opportunity to switch your selection."

The students and teachers murmured and whispered.

"So, Rodman," continued Principal Marshall. "What's it going to be: envelope number one, envelope number two, or envelope number three?"

The perspiration soaked right through Rodman's tee shirt and dress shirt. He had never been so nervous in all his life. He wished that he had a favorite number or some system to help guide him to make the proper choice. The students were trying to assist him by shouting out which envelope to pick, but this was no help. What did they know? Weren't their guesses every bit as random as his? After several moments of contemplation, Rodman finally lifted his hand with one finger pointing straight up. "I pick envelope number one." A third of the audience erupted in wild applause.

After allowing the crowd to settle back down, Principal Marshall asked Rodman if he was sure. Rodman, very unsure, nodded his head and said yes.

"So, number one it is," said the principal. "As promised, I will try to make your chances a little better by eliminating one of the wrong envelopes. You chose envelope number one. I am willing to tell you that the 1,000 dollars is definitely *not* in envelope number three."

To prove this, Principal Marshall walked to the corkboard and opened the third envelope. He removed a picture of Morey Holland smiling and wearing a birthday hat, and pinned it to the board. "Now, as promised, I am going to give you one more option. You can either stick with envelope number one, or you can switch to envelope number two. What will it be?"

Rodman sank into a deep thinking trance. Despite the shouts of the crowd, he could only hear his own thoughts. He knew that this was a critical decision. As intensely as he could, he contemplated the following:

If I switch my selection from envelope number one to envelope number two, will my chances for picking the 1,000 dollars increase, decrease, or stay exactly the same? (*Solution on page 102.*)

Conclusion

And so ends the story of the case of the stolen exams. Rodman saved the day and won 1,000 dollars. But will he ever find his way around the school? Will he ever find the courage to speak to Ashleigh Ray? More importantly, will he ever be able to make it through a day without being involved in a ridiculous probability puzzle? The odds are three to one against him.

SOLUTIONS

1: THE RACQUET BROTHERS (PAGE 7)

A little "lateral thinking" is all that is needed to solve this first brainteaser. Born of the same parents on the exact same day of the exact same year, Bill and Nick Racquet were not twins—*they were two of a set of triplets.*

2: TRUE OR FALSE (PAGE 9)

Here's the problem: If V.P. Magnesium asked Bill, the truthful brother, which key would open the lock, he would point to the correct key. But if Nick, the lying brother, was asked the same question, he would surely point to the wrong key. Since the vice principal couldn't distinguish which brother was truthful, asking this question would not resolve the key dilemma.

The challenge was for V.P. Magnesium to come up with a question that would identify the proper key—no matter which brother was asked. Although this dilemma can be solved in different ways, V.P. Magnesium came up with this:

If I asked your brother which was the correct key, what would he answer?

If the truthful brother was asked this question, he would point to the *wrong key*, since that is the key his lying brother would indicate.

And if the lying brother was asked, he would also point to the wrong key. Can you see why? It's because he is a liar, and the *wrong key* is the opposite of what his truthful brother would have answered.

So no matter which brother was asked, he would point to the wrong key. This way, V.P. Magnesium knew to use the *opposite key* from what was indicated to open the door to the computer lab. Here's another possible solution:

If I asked you yesterday which was the correct key, what would you have said?

Of course, Bill, the truthful brother, would point to the correct key, since that was what he would have said yesterday. And the liar, Nick, would also point to the correct key. Why? Because *yesterday*, Nick would have answered with a lie and pointed to the wrong key. But since Nick was asked which key he would have pointed to *yesterday*, he would lie and point to the correct key! Does this make sense?   Is your head spinning?

The solution to many truth-versus-lie brainteasers calls for asking a compound question, forcing the liar to turn his lie around.

3: RODMAN PILGRIM (PAGE 11)

Four students are in Mrs. Turkus's second-period AP English class: Fran, Gilbert, Peter, and Gordon. There are five desks. Rodman's goal is to identify the vacant desk. Here are the facts:

1. Fran is not at desk number 1.
2. Gilbert sits next to the empty desk.
3. Fran is two desks away from Peter.
4. Fran sits next to the empty desk.
5. Peter sits at desk number 4.

Let's go through Rodman's reasoning process so that we can see how he identified his seat:

To begin with, clue #5 tells us that Peter is at the fourth desk.

Peter

According to clue #3, Fran sits two desks away from Peter. And the second desk is the only one that is two desks away from Peter. This also satisfies clue #1 that Fran is not at the first desk.

Clue #4 tells us that Fran's desk is next to the vacant desk, so Rodman must sit at either the first desk or the third desk.

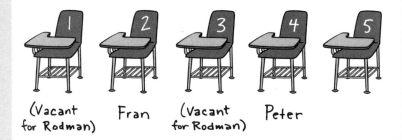

(Vacant for Rodman)   Fran   (Vacant for Rodman)   Peter

This leaves us with the final clue, #2: Gilbert sits next to an empty desk. But wait a minute. I believe we have run into a snag. If Fran is at the second desk and Peter is at the fourth desk, how could Gilbert possibly sit next to an empty seat? In our chart, there do not appear to be two vacant seats next to each other. But how can this be? We followed all of the clues. Unless ...

Unless the desks are not situated in a row. *Maybe they are positioned in a circle.*

Now, that would open our chart to other possibilities. Run through the clues again: Clue #5 says that Peter sits at the fourth desk.

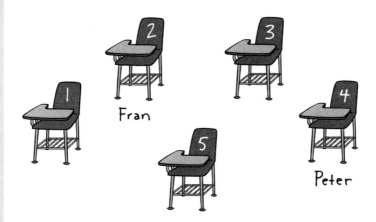

Clue #3 says that Fran sits two desks away from Peter. This means that she sits either at the first desk (going clockwise) or the second desk (going counterclockwise). But clue #1 says that Fran does not sit at the first desk; therefore, Fran sits at the second desk.

Clue #2 tells us that Gilbert sits next to an empty seat (which will be Rodman's seat). The only way this could be possible is if there are two open seats next to each other in our chart—which there are: seats 1 and 5. So, seats 1 and 5 are taken by Gilbert and Rodman, which means that the only seat left for Gordon is the third one.

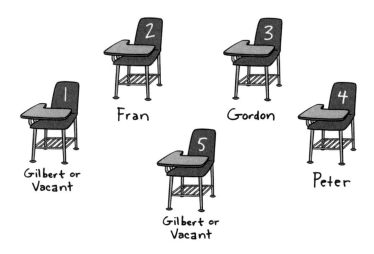

And since clue #4 says that Fran sits next to an empty desk, Gilbert must sit at the fifth desk, leaving the first position open to Rodman. The final chart is as follows:

4: A SAFE SOLUTION (PAGE 14)

The challenge was to determine the least number of locks and keys needed to allow any two of the three people to open the safe and prevent any one person from opening the safe alone.

The answer is three locks and six keys (two for each person). Here's why:

Let's call the three locks A, B, and C. The keys would be distributed as follows:

- The teacher gets the keys to locks A and B.
- Alex gets the keys to locks B and C.
- Rudy gets the keys to locks A and C.

As you can see, any two of them could open the safe together, but none of them could open it alone.

5: THERMOS BE A BETTER WAY (PAGE 19)

The class was working with three thermoses in the following sizes: 7 ounces, 9 ounces, and 11 ounces. Their goal was to make exactly 10 ounces of coffee, while wasting as little as possible. The best solution the class could devise involved wasting 6 ounces. Mrs. Cook asked the class to do better.

Much to the dismay of Mrs. Cook, her students were not able to decrease the amount of wasted coffee. Perhaps if Rodman had made it to the class on time, he would have been able to show Mrs. Cook how to fix exactly 10 ounces and waste only 4. Although there are several ways to make this happen, here is one solution: Fill the 7-ouncer and dump it directly into the 9-ouncer. Then refill the 7-ouncer:

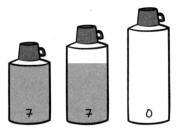

From the 7-ouncer, fill up the 9-ouncer (adding only 2 ounces) and pour the remainder (5 ounces) into the 11-ouncer:

From the 9-ouncer, fill the 7-ouncer (leaving 2 ounces in the 9-ouncer). Then take the 7-ouncer and cap off the 11-ouncer (leaving 1 ounce in the 7-ouncer):

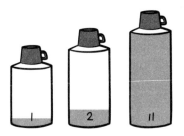

Pour the 2 ounces from the 9-ouncer into the 7-ouncer (making 3 ounces total). From the 11-ouncer, fill up the 9-ouncer (leaving 2 ounces in the 11-ouncer):

Dump the 2 ounces from the 11-ouncer down the sink. Move the 3 ounces from the 7-ouncer to the 11-ouncer:

From the 9-ouncer, fill the 7-ouncer (leaving 2 ounces in the 9-ouncer). Then dump the full contents from the 7-ouncer into the 11-ouncer:

And then dump the 2 remaining ounces down the sink, wasting a total of just 4 ounces.

6: THE BOILER ROOM (PAGE 26)

Of course, there was a better solution than Mr. Pock's crackpot wild goose chase upstairs. There were three light switches and three light bulbs. The challenge was to figure out a way to determine which switch controlled which light. Mr. Magnesium came up with this plan:

Turn on switch 1, wait 10 minutes, and then turn it off. Turn on switch 2, and then walk upstairs to his office. The light bulb that is on is controlled by switch 2. The light bulb that is warm is controlled by switch 1. And the light bulb that is room temperature is controlled by switch 3.

7: OH BOY! (PAGE 29)

Miss Stewart said that since they already knew that one of the two students was a boy, then the chances that the other student was a girl were two out of three (two-thirds). Apparently, Miss Stewart was thinking of this classic brainteaser:

A mother has exactly two children. At least one is a boy. What is the probability that the other child is a girl?

This question has been the source of many intense arguments, heated debates, and screaming matches. Brilliant minds disagree over the solution to this perplexing conundrum. Mathematicians, professors, and other great thinkers will say the answer is either one-half or two-thirds, depending upon how the question is interpreted. But let's see how this brainteaser applies to the case of the stolen exams. Is there, as Miss Stewart claims, a two-thirds chance that the other student is a girl?

Unfortunately for Miss Stewart, she was way off in this instance. The situation at Riddle Middle School is different than that of the mother with two children. In the middle school, there is a fixed number of boys and girls. This fact allows us to figure out the solution a different way. We know that one of the culprits has to be a boy. If we assume that there are an equal number of boys and girls in the school, then there is virtually a 50 percent chance that the other student is a girl.

8: THE CLASS LIST (PAGE 36)

When the principal calculated how many pairs could be made with 8 students, he forgot that you couldn't count the same pair twice. If you count the pair Rudy/Ashleigh, you couldn't count Ashleigh/Rudy as a separate pair, so 64 pairs is wrong. It is not clear what was behind Mr. Magnesium's reasoning, but 16 pairs is clearly wrong as well. This was Mr. Pock's thinking:

The first student would be able to make pairs with each of the other 7 students. The second student would be able to be paired with the remaining 6 students (but not with the first student, since that pair was already counted!). The third student could be paired with the remaining 5 students, and so forth.

In total, we would have 7 + 6 + 5 + 4 + 3 + 2 + 1 = 28 pairs.

9: B OR BETTER (PAGE 38)

Okay. Let's all calm down and take a deep breath. I know that this is a really hard one, but if you stick with me and take it one step at a time, you will see how it all makes sense in the end.

To recap, the students had to figure out if they had a B average or better. They could see everyone else's grades on the index card, but not their own. As soon as the poorer performers realize their grades are less than a B, they are to stop coming to class. As a reminder, here are the students' grades for the year:

Fran: A   Gordon: B   Rodman: B
Peter: C   Gilbert: C

Well, it looks like Peter and Gilbert will get the boot out of the AP class as soon as they realize they did not make the grade. But how will they come to this conclusion? To answer this, let's take a step backwards and pretend that instead of two students having below a B, there was only one: Gilbert.

If this were the case, then Gilbert would look at the grades on the index card and see that *everyone else had a grade of B or better*. And since Mrs. Turkus stated that at least one student didn't make the grade, Gilbert would think that he must be the only student who did not hit the mark. Realizing this, he would not come to class the next morning.

So far, so good? Great! Hang in there, because this next part gets a little thorny.

Well, Gilbert was not the only student whose grade fell below a B. Gilbert and Peter both missed the mark. Since this was the case:

Gilbert would have seen that
Fran, Gordon, and Rodman all had a B or higher
and Peter didn't reach a B.
Peter would have seen that
Fran, Gordon, and Rodman all had a B or higher
and Gilbert didn't reach a B.

We're almost there! Stay with me . . .

Gilbert and Peter each saw on the index card that someone's grade had fallen below a B, so they would both show up to class the next day. Why? Because they knew that at least one person's grade fell below a B, and since they each saw that someone else had a grade below a B, they had no reason to think—at that point—that they also had a grade below a B. They each had expected the other not to show up the next day.

But when Gilbert and Peter saw each other in class the next day, they each had to think, *Uh oh! He is here! That must mean he saw someone else on the list who had a grade below a B, or else he would not have shown up! And, since I can see everyone else scored a B or higher, that must mean it was me who didn't hit the mark! Yikes!*

This being the case, both Gilbert and Peter would not report to class on the second day after being given the challenge, realizing that the two of them didn't score a B or better.

So, in our scenario . . .

It would take two days for Gilbert and Peter to stop coming to class.

It would take two days for two people to stop coming to class. The same principle would apply for three, four, or five people (or more, had there been more students in the class). The answer will always correspond with the number of people who didn't reach the mark. If three students had fallen below a B, then it would have taken three days for the students to stop coming; if it had been 700 students, it would have taken 700 days; and so forth.

10: THE BIRTHDAY MIRACLE (PAGE 43)

So, a student shares a birthday with Morey Holland. Is this a miracle, as Morey claims, or just a coincidence, as Molly suggests?

To begin with, it seems that Morey and Molly were discussing different issues entirely. Morey was amazed by the fact that someone in such a small class shared *his* birthday, and Molly was saying that it was not unusual for two people—any two people—to share a birthday in a classroom. Let's start with Molly's point of view. It was a mathematician named Richard von Mises who, in 1939, posed the following question (paraphrased):

What is the minimum number of people needed to be in a room for there to be at least a 50 percent chance that two people (any two people in the room) share a birthday?

How many did you guess? A hundred, two hundred, more? Let's take a closer look to see if we can come up with an exact number. If Morey walked into a room with only one student in it, the probability of the two of them having matching birthdays would be 1 in 365 (or 364 to 1). If there were two students and Morey, then the chances would be much better, because *any two* of the three could match: Morey could match with either student, or the two students could match with each other! If we added yet another student, then the possible combinations for matching birthdays would increase greatly. Even with as few as 10 people in the room, there is almost a 12 percent chance that two of them would have matching birthdays.

So how many people do we need to make it likely that two people share a birthday? The answer seems to shock most people: 23. With as few as 23 people in a room, the odds are slightly greater than 50 percent that two people (any two) would share a birthday. (Coincidentally, 23 is the exact number of people who were in Morey Holland's drama class.) And the odds increase greatly with each additional person. With 30 people, the odds are 70 percent; 50 people would give us a 97 percent chance; and 60 people would almost guarantee a match, with the odds at 99 percent! In fact, if there were 100 people, the odds would be more than a million to one that there would be at least one birthday match in the room.

Of course, this is only valid for a 365-day year. Surprisingly, if you figure in the extra day in a leap year, the odds do not change much—23 is still the magic number for a 366-day year.

If you tried this at a party with 30 to 40 people, you would be able to amaze most of the guests. Most people would not believe that it is likely to have a birthday match with so few people. In fact, many people I have asked think that there needs to be at least 300 people—sometimes as much as 500 people—in a room to make it likely that two people would have matching birthdays.

Any answer higher than 367 is clearly a wild guess. If there were 367 people in a room, a birthday match would be *guaranteed*—100 percent—even in a leap year! And we asked for only a 50 percent chance.

So it seems that Molly Peltin was right. With 23 people in the room, it was hardly a miracle that two people would have matching birthdays. But Morey Holland wasn't concerned about other people matching—he was marveling at the fact that someone's birthday matched *his*.

He claimed that in a room of 22 students, the odds would be 365 to 22 that his birthday would match someone else's. Then according to Morey's theory, there would need to be 183 people in the room for it to be likely that someone's birthday would match *his* birthday. Is he right?

He is actually way off. Because it is possible for some (or all) of the students to have the same birthday as each other, we would need many more than 183 people to give Morey a greater than 50 percent chance of matching birthdays. Morey probably would have thought that his birthday match was much more of a miracle if he had known that there would need to be at least 253 people in the room to make it likely that someone shared his birthday.

As an interesting note, if you were to ask the same question for identical or adjacent birthdays (any two people matching the exact day or within one day), all you would need is 14 people in the room for the odds to be in favor of a match.

11: THE MISSING DOLLAR (PAGE 46)

This is a perfect example of misleading mathematics—or a trick question—because a dollar really isn't missing. By the way the problem was presented, there only *appears* to be a missing dollar.

Hy said that his mother gave him 20 dollars. He gave her back 3 dollars, which means that she ended up spending a total of 17 dollars. Hy also purchased candy bars for 2 dollars. He was confused because 17 + 2 = 19 and not 20. But there is no reason on earth to add 17 and 2.

If you want to use math to solve this problem, you would calculate the following: The cat bowl cost 15 dollars, the candy bars cost 2 dollars, and there was 3 dollars' change. 15 + 2 + 3 = 20. Or, if you prefer: Hy started with 20 dollars, spent 15 dollars on the cat bowl and 2 dollars on the candy bars, and had 3 dollars' change. 20 – 15 – 2 = 3. No missing dollar. What Hy did was idiotic and only served to confuse his friend Wilson. It's a good thing Rodman was there to save the day.

12: THREE AMIGOS, A JANITOR, AND AN ELEVATOR (PAGE 50)

The challenge was to come up with a solution that would not allow two of the Three Amigos to be alone with the safe at any time. Let's see how Mr. Pock solved this dilemma:

First trip down: Mr. Pock brings Mr. Raccoon down and leaves him and the safe alone in the lobby.

First trip up: Mr. Pock rides up the elevator alone.

Second trip down: Mr. Pock brings Rudy down, leaving Alex by himself on the second floor.

Second trip up: Mr. Pock leaves Rudy in the lobby and brings Mr. Raccoon and the safe back up with him.

Third trip down Mr. Pock deposits Mr. Raccoon on the second floor and brings down Alex.

Third trip up: Mr. Pock goes up alone, leaving the two students alone in the school lobby.

Fourth trip down: Mr. Pock escorts Mr. Raccoon and the safe down to where the two students are waiting.

This solution successfully transported both students and Mr. Raccoon without giving two of them an opportunity to open the safe without the third. Bravo, Mr. Pock!

13: THEY'RE CLOSING IN (PAGE 54)

The note given to Mr. Marshall indicated that at least one of the two students was a boy. This eliminates girl/girl pairs as suspects:

Rudy/Fran   Rudy/Ashleigh   Rudy/Alex   Rudy/Wilson
Rudy/Lori-Beth   Rudy/Molly   Rudy/Hy   Fran/Alex
Fran/Wilson   Fran/Hy   Ashleigh/Alex   Ashleigh/Wilson
Ashleigh/Hy   Alex/Wilson   Alex/Lori-Beth   Alex/Molly
Alex/Hy   Wilson/Lori-Beth   Wilson/Molly   Wilson/Hy
Lori-Beth/Hy   Molly/Hy

Mr. Marshall also told his staff that one of the two students must have had an A in computers. The four students with A's were Rudy, Wilson, Lori-Beth, and Molly. This means that only the pairs with one or more of these A students can remain:

RudyFran   Rudy/Ashleigh   Rudy/Alex   Rudy/Wilson
Rudy/Lori-Beth   Rudy/Molly   Rudy/Hy   Fran/Wilson
Ashleigh/Wilson   Alex/Wilson   Alex/Lori-Beth   Alex/Molly
Wilson/Lori-Beth   Wilson/Molly   Wilson/Hy   Lori-Beth/Hy
Molly/Hy

Not bad. Mr. Marshall and his staff were able to reduce the pairs of suspects from 28 to 17. They're closing in!

14: TO TELL THE TRUTH (PAGE 58)

Mr. Marshall had ordered Rudy to make a statement. If the statement were true, Rudy would receive five days of detention. If it were false, then he would be suspended for five days . Rudy was able to come up with a statement that would get him off the hook completely. He said:

"I am going to be suspended."

Mr. Marshall was dumfounded. He couldn't suspend Rudy because if he did, then Rudy's statement would have ended up being true. He could suspend Rudy only if his statement was a lie.

Mr. Marshall was also unable to give Rudy detention. This is because the only way that Rudy could get detention is if he made a true statement. And "I am going to be suspended" would have been a lie if he had gotten detention!

15: INKREDIBLE DISCOVERY (PAGE 63)

The primary goal of the principal and the department heads was to find the midterm exams without being sprayed with the permanent ink. Since the three boxes were all intentionally labeled incorrectly, it was impossible to figure out which box contained the exams without the risk of opening a wrong box first. Although the principal and the department heads would not enjoy being splattered with snake poop, they were willing to risk that possibility. They only wanted to avoid the ink. So, here was Rodman's solution:

Open the box labeled PERMANENT INK. The principal's assessment that they had a 33 percent of guessing the right box on the first try was incorrect. Since they knew that the boxes were all labeled incorrectly, they could be sure that the ink box did not contain ink. It contained either the snake poop or the midterm exams, giving them a 50 percent chance of success. If they opened the ink box and found the tests, their search was over. And if the ink box contained snake poop, then that would leave two boxes: SNAKE POOP and MIDTERM EXAMS. Since all three of the boxes were all labeled incorrectly, they knew that the tests could not be in the MIDTERM EXAMS box, so they would have to be in the SNAKE POOP box.

16: AND THEN THERE WERE TWO (PAGE 68)

We have already been able to reduce the field of suspects from 28 possible pairs to just 17 (see Challenge # 13, page 54).

The remaining 17 pairs can also be shaved down once we look at the clues more closely. The note that was given to the principal said, "Me and my friend have stolen all of the midterm exams!"

All of you sleuths reading this would have picked up that the key word in that sentence was "friend." This means that the two culprits are friends with each other. Why is this significant? Well, in Chapter 5 (Thermos Be a Better Way), we learned that Lori-Beth Sugarman ". . . did not have a single friend in the entire school." Since Lori-Beth had no friends, it completely eliminates her from the possible suspects; therefore, we can cross off every pair that includes Lori-Beth from our list. That leaves us with the following pairs:

Rudy/Fran   Rudy/Ashleigh   Rudy/Alex   Rudy/Wilson
Rudy/Molly   Rudy/Hy   Fran/Wilson   Ashleigh/Wilson
Alex/Wilson   Alex/Molly   Wilson/Molly   Wilson/Hy
Molly/Hy

In 11 (The Missing Dollar, page 46), we learned that poor Wilson didn't ever speak to girls. But what's bad news for Wilson is good news for us, because it allows us to cross off any combination that matched Wilson with a girl. So let's see what pairs are left:

Rudy/Fran   Rudy/Ashleigh   Rudy/Alex   Rudy/Wilson
Rudy/Molly   Rudy/Hy   Alex/Wilson   Alex/Molly   Wilson/Hy
Molly/Hy

We can also find a clue in 10 (The Birthday Miracle, page 43), when we met our youngest suspect, Molly Peltin. All pairs that include Molly can be eliminated because she is a seventh-grader, and we know that the theft was committed by two eighth-graders. This leaves us with just these pairs:

Rudy/Fran   Rudy/Ashleigh   Rudy/Alex   Rudy/Wilson   Rudy/Hy
Alex/Wilson   Wilson/Hy

Well, well, well. It's not looking so great for Rudy. Out of the last seven pairs, he figures prominently in five of them. Do you remember meeting Rudy Wichter? He was the student who was involved with that "candy in the safe" scandal. You may recall something about Rudy that will help us reduce our list of suspects even further. Rudy is on the school basketball team, and he had sprained both of his hands diving for a loose ball a couple of weeks earlier. His hands and fingers were in hard plastic casts, completely bandaged. This would have made it impossible for him to either hack into the computer or write the note to the principal. So we can eliminate all pairs that feature Rudy. Now we are left with just these two:

Alex/Wilson   Wilson/Hy

Alex and Wilson or Wilson and Hy. Well, it looks as if we found half of our duo. Wilson stole the midterm exams with either Alex or Hy. So which one is it? Well we already know that Wilson and Hy are friends (*see Challenge 11, The Missing Dollar*); and we also learned that Wilson does not like anyone who is on a school sports team. Alex was on the school basketball team with Rudy. This leaves us with only one remaining pair of suspects: *Wilson and Hy*!

17: THE STUDENTS' DILEMMA (PAGE 69)

Will the pact made by Wilson and Hy hold up? Or will they fold under the pressure and confess? Each student must decide if he wants to do what is best for the pair or for himself. To help us see if the boys are likely to confess, let's go over Mr. Marshall's deal in detail. There are three possible punishments:

1. Expulsion from school (harshest punishment)
2. Detention until the end of the year (medium punishment)
3. Detention for one month (lightest punishment)

And there are three possible outcomes:

1. If both students remain silent: They each get the lightest punishment.
2. If one student confesses and the other remains silent: The confessor goes free and the other student gets the harshest punishment.
3. If both students confess: They each get the medium punishment.

Even though neither student will know what the other has decided, he will have to examine the possible outcomes. Here is what Wilson is thinking:

Option A: I confess (I get one day of suspension and one month of detention) If Hy confesses or Option B: I remain silent (I get one month of detention).

So Wilson concludes: "If Hy confesses, then it looks like my best bet is to confess! But what if Hy remains silent?"

Option A: I confess (I go free!).
If Hy remains silent or
Option B: I remain silent (I get one month of detention).

So Wilson concludes: "Well, what do you know about that! If Hy remains silent, then I am still better off if I confess."

This is the realization that the students will most likely come to: *It is always in my best interest to confess—no matter what my partner does*.

This puzzle is a variation on a classic problem developed by Merrill Flood and Melvin Dresher in 1950 and then adapted by mathematician Albert W. Tucker in a version he called the "Prisoner's Dilemma." It has been studied by businessmen, economists, politicians, generals, and game theorists.

This game/dilemma becomes more interesting if the two players (suspects) are allowed to take this challenge repeatedly. If Hy and Wilson were faced with this decision every week, the results would be different. Once each player sees how the other responds, he can decide whether or not to cooperate in the future. Experts who study this game/dilemma generally agree that the smartest way to play is to always do what your opponent did the time before. This would eventually teach the other player that it is really in his or her best interest to keep the pact and remain silent each time. Overall, this method will produce the least amount of punishment for both players over the entire course of the game.

18: SURPRISE, SURPRISE! (PAGE 73)

Theoretically, Wilson has a point. He believes that since the day their detentions begin will come as a surprise, then the detentions can never happen at all. Here's why:

Next week consists of Monday, Tuesday, Wednesday, Thursday, and Friday. Well, if Thursday rolls around and detention did not start by then, that would mean that detention would *definitely* start on Friday, since that's the only day left—and that wouldn't surprise Wilson and Hy at all! Thus, detention cannot start on Friday.

Since Friday has been eliminated, the only days detention can start are Monday, Tuesday, Wednesday, and Thursday. If Wednesday comes and detention has not started, then they would know for certain that detention would have to start on Thursday—since that's the only possible day left—and that wouldn't be a surprise. That means detention cannot possibly start on Thursday.

So that leaves Monday, Tuesday, and Wednesday. Can you see where this is going? If detention hadn't started by Tuesday, then the only day left would be Wednesday—and then that would not come as a surprise. That means detention cannot possibly start on Wednesday.

Now only Monday and Tuesday are left. If detention doesn't start on Monday, then it would have to start on Tuesday—and that would not be a surprise. So detention cannot start on Tuesday.

That leaves only Monday. Monday is the only day that detention could possibly start, since all of the other days have been eliminated. And since they have figured that out, it is not a surprise. That means detention cannot start on Monday.

Yes, Wilson has figured out that detention can never come because it could never be a surprise! So imagine Wilson's amazement when Mr. Marshall tapped him on the shoulder on Tuesday morning and told him detention started that day. *Surprise!*

19: RODMAN'S CHOICE (PAGE 75)

This brainteaser was derived from a game show called *Let's Make a Deal* that was enormously popular in the 1960s and 1970s. Hosted by the lovable and slick-talking Monty Hall, this program offered guests chances to earn prizes and then attempt to improve their lots by wheeling and dealing with the host.

On the surface this appears to be a ridiculously easy puzzle. Virtually 100 percent of the people who attempt to solve this brainteaser will say that Rodman has *exactly the same* chance of winning if he stays with his original selection (envelope number one) or switches to envelope number two. Their reason is that since there are two envelopes left, each envelope has a 50 percent chance of containing the grand prize.

This logic sounds reasonable, but to think that each envelope has a 50 percent chance of containing the 1,000 dollars is 100 percent wrong. The correct answer is that Rodman would have a *significantly greater chance of winning the grand prize if he switches to envelope number two*.

Go ahead, make a weird face. Tell me I'm crazy. Get it out of your system. When you are ready for the explanation, take a deep breath and prepare to be convinced.

PROOF THAT I'M NOT OUT OF MY MIND

Are you thinking that if Rodman sticks with envelope number one then he has a 50 percent chance of winning the grand prize since there are now only two envelopes remaining? That would be wrong. His odds remain one-third. Let's see why.

I would like you to pretend that you were presented Rodman's challenge 12 times. For the sake of this explanation, let's assume that you chose envelope number one each time. Let's also assume that you *never* switched envelopes. Statistically speaking, how many of the 12 chances will envelope number one contain the grand prize? Did you come up with 4? You should have, since statistically you will be correct one-third of the time, and one-third of 12 is 4. *Statistically, if you never switch, you will select the correct envelope 4 times out of 12 chances.*

So far, so good. If any of that is confusing, reread it before going further. Now let's take a look at two charts.

Never Switch

Statistically, out of 12 chances, envelope number one will be correct 4 times (one-third). To be fair, let's have each of the three envelopes win one-third of the time. Remember, Principal Marshall will always eliminate one of the wrong choices before giving Rodman the chance to switch. Here is the probable outcome if you *never switched* envelopes:

Selection	Eliminated Envelope	Winning Envelope	Win/Lose
1	2	1	Win
1	2	1	Win
1	3	1	Win
1	3	1	Win
1	3	2	Lose
1	3	2	Lose
1	3	2	Lose
1	3	2	Lose
1	2	3	Lose
1	2	3	Lose
1	2	3	Lose
1	2	3	Lose

See what happened? If you *never switched* from envelope number one, you would have selected the correct envelope only 4 out of 12 times. So, you would not have picked the correct envelope half of the time as you had initially thought! You would have been correct only one-third of the time.

But! Using the same scenario (which is statistically correct), if you *always switched*, look at how many times you would have won:

Always Switch

Do you see? If you *always switch*, you have a two-out-of-three chance of selecting the correct envelope. You would have won 8 times! But if you *never switched*, your odds would remain at one-third and you would have won only 4 times.

Selection	Eliminated Envelope	Switch to:	Winning Envelope	Win/Lose
1	2	3	1	Lose
1	2	3	1	Lose
1	3	2	1	Lose
1	3	2	1	Lose
1	3	2	2	Win
1	3	2	2	Win
1	3	2	2	Win
1	2	2	2	Win
1	2	3	3	Win
1	2	3	3	Win
1	2	3	3	Win
1	2	3	3	Win

Index

Note: Page references to solutions are in **bold.**

About the Author

ROBERT MANDELBERG is the author of *The Case of the Curious Campaign* and several mind-reading books. One of his plays, *You're Nobody Until Somebody Kills You,* has toured nationally, and his movie short, *Death Row,* has appeared in film festivals throughout the United States. Robert Lives with his wife, Nika, and his daughter, Eliana, in Monmouth County, New Jersey.

To learn more about Robert's upcoming projects visit his Web site at
www.RobertMandelberg.com